# 101 C++ Programming Challenges

### First Edition

**Yashavant Kanetkar**
**Aditya Kanetkar**

**FIRST EDITION 2017**

Copyright © BPB Publications, INDIA
ISBN :978-93-8655-159-7

**Distributors:**

**BPB PUBLICATIONS** 20,
Ansari Road, Darya Ganj
New Delhi-110002
Ph: 23254990/23254991

**COMPUTER BOOK CENTRE**
12, Shrungar Shopping Centre,
M.G.Road, BENGALURU–560001
Ph: 25587923/25584641

**BPB BOOK CENTRE**
376 Old Lajpat Rai Market,
Delhi-110006
Ph: 23861747

**DECCAN AGENCIES**
4-3-329, Bank Street,
Hyderabad-500195
Ph: 24756967/24756400

**MICRO MEDIA**
Shop No. 5, Mahendra Chambers, 150 DN
Rd. Next to Capital Cinema, V.T. (C.S.T.)
Station, MUMBAI-400 001 Ph:
22078296/22078297

Published by Manish Jain for BPB Publications, 20, Ansari Road, Darya Ganj, New Delhi-110002 and Printed him at Repro India Pvt Ltd, Mumbai

*We know that you are here with us*
*on this day...*

## About Yashavant Kanetkar

 Through his books and Quest Courseware DVDs on C, C++, Java, .NET, Embedded Systems, etc. Yashavant Kanetkar has created, moulded and groomed lacs of IT careers in the last two decades. Yashavant's books and Quest DVDs have made a significant contribution in creating top-notch IT manpower in India and abroad.

Yashavant's books are globally recognized and millions of students / professionals have benefitted from them. Yashavant's books have been translated into Hindi, Gujarati, Japanese, Korean and Chinese languages. Many of his books are published in India, USA, Japan, Singapore, Korea and China.

Yashavant is a much sought after speaker in the IT field and has conducted seminars/workshops at TedEx, IITs, RECs and global software companies.

Yashavant has recently been honored with the prestigious "Distinguished Alumnus Award" by IIT Kanpur for his entrepreneurial, professional and academic excellence. This award was given to top 50 alumni of IIT Kanpur who have made significant contribution towards their profession and betterment of society in the last 50 years.

In recognition of his immense contribution to IT education in India, he has been awarded the "Best .NET Technical Contributor" and "Most Valuable Professional" awards by Microsoft for 5 successive years.

Yashavant holds a BE from VJTI Mumbai and M.Tech. from IIT Kanpur.

## About Aditya Kanetkar

 Aditya Kanetkar holds a Master's Degree in Computer Science from Georgia Tech, Atlanta. Prior to that, he completed his Bachelor's Degree in Computer Science and Engineering from IIT Guwahati. He is currently working as a Software Engineer at Oracle America Inc. at Redwood City, California.

Aditya is a very keen programmer since his intern days at Redfin, Amazon Inc. and Arista Networks. His current passion is anything remotely connected to Java Technologies, Android programming and Databases.

# Preface

Most C++ programmers are former C programmers. Irrespective of amount of time that they may have spent doing C programming, when they migrate to C++ programming there is a huge paradigm shift. More than the syntax, it is the way one thinks about the program that has to change. One has to think in Object-Oriented manner. You may cry from rooftop saying that since the world is full of objects, so also should a program be, and your thinking should revolve around objects. Unfortunately, though natural, it is easier said than done. Unless one spends enough time figuring out why a particular object-oriented feature has been introduced in C++, you end up doing C programming with a C++ compiler.

Added to that is the fact that most C++ programming books consume a lot of pages explaining the concept, but when it comes to putting that concept into action the example programs are found wanting. There seems to be more of a pained effort to bring in the feature into the program rather than a natural need. Also, the exercises in many C++ books appear to be quite rudimentary in nature. As a result, they are found inadequate in testing the knowledge and competence of the reader in C++ programming.

We hope that this book would fill that void. Not only have we put together 101 Challenges in C++ programming, we have also organized them according to features of C++ programming one needs to use to solve them. If you are not able to solve a challenge or need a hint to solve it, there are ready-made solutions to each of the 101 challenges. In addition, the book also shows sample runs of these solutions, so that you get to know what input to give and what output to expect while solving a challenge. Each challenge is also followed up by a crisp explanation about the vital issues in the program solution. We hope you would find this aspect of the book—of putting everything about a challenge together—quite useful. We have also used illustrative icons to highlight the Challenge, Solution, Sample Run and Explanation so that you have no difficulty in spotting them.

So using this book not only would you be able to hone your programming skills, but also become a more mature C++ programmer.

We urge you to solve all the challenges in the book before migrating to learning other languages or technologies. If you do so you would be on much surer grounds while learning them.

All the best and happy programming!

**Yashavant Kanetkar**

**Aditya Kanetkar**

# Challenges

# 01/ Total Challenges: 7

# Getting Off The Ground Challenges

**P**eople say that learning programming and related technologies is a moving target. Technologies continue to evolve and to harness their power to create solutions, languages need to come up with updated versions. C++ is no different in this regard. One must remain updated about these developments as new features can help solve the same problem more elegantly, than the quirky way in which it was being solved with earlier versions. This chapter will help you keep abreast with these developments.

## Challenge  01

Are there multiple versions of C++ language? Which is the latest version?

## Solution

C++ was developed by Bjarne Stroustrup at Bell Labs since 1979. It was planned as an extension of the C language to help improve program organization. In fact, to begin with it was named as "C with Classes". It had features like classes, inheritance, strong type-checking and default values for function arguments.

In 1983, "C with Classes" was renamed to "C++". New features like virtual functions, function overloading, operator overloading, references, constants, type-safe free-store memory allocation (new/delete), improved type checking, and // style comments.

Once it started becoming popular amongst programmers a need for its standardization was felt. The standardization of C++ is done by an ISO (International Organization for Standardization) working group known as JTC1/SC22/WG21. The first standard was released in 1998 and came to be known as C++98.

In 2003, it published a new version of the C++ standard, which essentially fixed problems identified in C++98.

The next major revision of the standard was released in 2011 and is known as C++11. It contained many additions to both the core language and the standard library.

In 2014, C++14 was released, which had bug fixes in C+11 and a few small improvements.

The group is currently working on the next revision of the standard which is slated for release in July 2017. C++20 is the next planned standard for future.

## Challenge 02

Which are the different ways to build a C++ program?

## Solution

You may either build the program using the command-line manually, or use a convenient Integrated Development Environment (IDE). IDEs internally make use of the same preprocessor, compiler, assembler, etc. that are used on command-line. Only thing is their usage remains hidden from the developer. For example, if we use the NetBeans IDE, it internally would internally use the same g++ compiler that is used for building the program on the command-line.

## Challenge 03

Are there any specific benefits in using an IDE for program development?

## Solution

Though C++ programs can be built using the command-line, using an Integrated Development Environments (IDEs) is preferred for the following reasons:

(a) All the program building steps like preprocessing, compilation, assembling, linking and execution can happen at the press of a button (for example, by using F6 function key in NetBeans IDE).

(b) IDE helps us manage all the project files through a "Project" or a "Solution Explorer" window. This is very useful for large projects which have multiple files in them.

(c) IDE provides easy navigation through the code stored in multiple files. For example, we can quickly find out from which different places in our code a particular function is being called.

(d) IDE displays line numbers besides each line of code.

(e)    IDE provides Syntax highlighting i.e. it shows keywords, functions, class names etc. in different colors making them stand out visually.

(f)    IDE provides code folding feature, where a piece of code can be collapsed / expanded as per the need. This is very helpful in managing large programs.

(g)    IDE lets us set bookmarks in code to help us quickly navigate to them quickly from other parts of the program.

(h)    IDE offers the Intellisense feature through which we can get help in the context in which we seek it. For example, when we type an object name it provides a list of functions that can be called using that object. Similarly, once we choose the function it provides the list of arguments that we need to pass to this function.

(i)    Once the compiler points out the errors, IDE provides suggestions as to how the error can be rectified.

(j)    For routine program statements like a for loop, a if - else structure etc. IDE provides readymade code blocks, thereby saving some typing effort.

(k)    IDE lets you add and manage non-programming resources like Icons, Bitmaps, Menus, Toolbars, etc. visually.

(l)    IDE provides vital statistics like build time, execution time etc. This can help us rate the performance of our program.

(m)    IDE provides a powerful editor through which we can rename token names throughout the project code in an efficient manner.

(n)    IDE provides visual debugging. We can see the break points that have been set, see the single stepping progress, watch values of variables / expressions, etc.

IDE provides many more such very useful features. In short it helps you in improving your programming efficiency and productivity.

## Challenge  04

Which IDEs can be used for building C++ programs?

## Solution

Three popular IDEs that are used for building C++ programs are as follows:

(a) NetBeans
(b) Eclipse
(c) Microsoft Visual Studio Code

All of them are free of cost and are available for Windows as well as Linux. Note that all of them are only IDEs and do not contain compiler or debugger tools. Often g++ compiler is used with NetBeans or Eclipse IDE.

Do not confuse between Microsoft Visual Studio Code and Visual Studio Professional. Visual Studio Code is an IDE that is available for Windows, Linux and Mac. However, it can be used to develop, test and deploy your programs within your internal corporate network only. For commercial development, Microsoft offers Visual Studio Professional or Visual Studio Enterprise as a subscription service.

Visual Studio subscription lets you create applications for multiple devices, PCs, and the web. With this subscription, cloud services are also available and development can be done for any of your preferred platforms and devices, including Windows, iOS, Android, and Linux.

A free toned-down version of Visual Studio is also available. It is called Visual Studio Express Edition. It can be downloaded from https://www.visualstudio.com/vs/visual-studio-express/.

## Challenge 05

Is it a good idea to use Turbo C++ for developing C++ programs?

## Solution

No. The reason being it was created for MS-DOS and is more than two decades old. It doesn't recognize many keywords and features that were later added to C++. These include templates, namespaces and exceptions.

## Challenge 06

What is the difference between gcc and g++ compilers?

## Solution

Firstly let us look at the long form of each.

GCC (in capitals): GNU Compiler Collection
gecko (in smallcase) : GNU C Compiler
g++: GNU C++ Compiler

GCC refers to compilers for different languages like C, C++, Fortran, Ada, etc. These include compilers gcc and g++. The main difference between gcc and g++ is as follows:

gcc compiles .c and .cpp files as C and C++ programs respectively. As against this, g++ compiles .c as well as .cpp files as if they are C++ programs.

## Challenge 07

Can we build C++ programs using the command-line? If yes, how?

## Solution

It is possible to build C++ programs using the command-line. Suppose we create and store the following program in a file "sample.cpp".

```
// sample.cpp
#include <iostream>
using namespace std ;

int main( )
{
    cout << "Some people are judged for being real..." << endl ;
```

```
    cout << "While others are loved for being fake." << endl ;
}
```

To build this program at Linux command-line using g++ compiler use the command

$ g++ sample.cpp -o output

The **-o** switch indicates that the executable code after building this program should be stored in a file called "output". Once the program has been built, to execute this output file use the command

$ ./output

The two messages in our program would now get displayed in the output.

Can we do the command-line building under Windows using Visual Studio compiler? The answer is yes. Here is the procedure.

Firstly, create a folder called "sample" and create "sample.cpp" shown above in this folder.

Visual C++ has complex requirements for the command-line environment in order to find the tools, headers, and libraries it uses. Hence we can't build the C++ program in a plain vanilla command prompt window. Fortunately, Visual Studio provides a developer command prompt that has the environment set up for command line builds. Unfortunately, the names of the developer command prompt shortcuts and where they are located are different in almost every version of Visual C++ and on different versions of Windows. So locate "Visual Studio Command Prompt" in your version of Visual Studio and Windows. Execute it and a command-prompt window would appear.

In the command window execute the following command to build the program:

C:\sample> cl sample.cpp

On successful build the executable code would be stored in sample.exe. Execute it using the command

C:\sample> sample

Once again the two messages in our program would be displayed on the screen.

# 02/ Total Ch

# The Starters Challenges

There are always multiple ways of solving the same C++ challenge. This chapter intends to use the incremental additions that have been done in C++, as compared to C, to help a programmer express his ideas better. For example, using flexible declarations, using bool data type, using enum instead of #defines, etc. This chapter provides solutions to challenges using such nuances.

## Challenge 08

In India the currency is made up of Rupee denominations Re. 1, Rs. 2, Rs. 5, Rs. 10, Rs. 50, Rs. 100, Rs. 500 and Rs. 2000.

A bank is trying to find the number of notes of each denomination that the teller can give a customer for a certain amount of money, such that he has to handle minimum number of notes. Write a program to list out the number of notes of each denomination for an amount received through the keyboard.

## Solution

```
// Project: chall08
// Program that tells the denomination and number of notes required to
// tender a particular amount
#include <iostream>
#include <iomanip>
using namespace std ;

void numtender ( int ) ;

int main( )
{
    int amount ;

    cout << "Enter the amount to be tendered: " << endl ;
    cin >> amount ;
    numtender ( amount ) ;

    return 0 ;
}

void numtender ( int amount )
{
    int den[ ] = { 1, 2, 5, 10, 20, 50, 100, 500, 2000 } ;
    int numofnotes ;

    if ( amount <= 0 )
```

```
        return ;

    cout << "Denomination details:" << endl ;
    for ( int i = 8 ; i >= 0 ; i-- )
    {
        if ( amount >= den[ i ] )
        {
            numofnotes = amount / den[ i ] ;
            cout << setw ( 4 ) << den[ i ] << " x "
                 << setw ( 3 ) << numofnotes << " = "
                 << setw ( 8 ) << den[ i ] * numofnotes << endl ;

            amount = amount % den[ i ] ;
            if ( amount == 0 )
                break ;
        }
    }
}
```

## Sample Runs

```
Enter the amount to be tendered:
12345
Denomination details:
2000  x   6  =   12000
 100  x   3  =     300
  20  x   2  =      40
   5  x   1  =       5

Enter the amount to be tendered:
23418
Denomination details:
2000  x  11  =   22000
 500  x   2  =    1000
 100  x   4  =     400
  10  x   1  =      10
   5  x   1  =       5
   2  x   1  =       2
   1  x   1  =       1
```

## Explanation

The program sets up an array **den[ ]** with all denomination values. Then through a **for** loop it finds out the number of notes required for each denomination beginning with the highest denomination, i.e. 2000. This order is important to ensure that the number of notes to be tendered are minimum.

Note the usage of **setw( )** manipulator. It right aligns the text to follow within the specified number of columns. Also, note the declaration of **i** within the **for** loop, instead of at the beginning of the function.

## Challenge  09

145 is a curious number, as 1! + 4! + 5! = 1 + 24 + 120 = 145.

Write a program to find all such numbers up to 10000 which are equal to the sum of the factorial of their digits.

## Solution

```cpp
// Project: chall09
// Program to find all curious numbers from 1 to 10000
#include <iostream>
using namespace std ;

int factorial ( int ) ;
bool isCurious ( int ) ;

int main( )
{
    cout << "List of curious numbers: " << endl ;
    for ( int i = 1 ; i <= 10000 ; i++ )
    {
        bool curious = isCurious ( i ) ;
        if ( curious == true )
            cout << i << endl ;
    }
    return 0 ;
```

```
}

int factorial ( int num )
{
    int p ;

    if ( num == 0 )
        return 1 ;
    else
        p = num * factorial ( num - 1 ) ;

    return p ;
}

bool isCurious ( int num )
{
    int sum = 0, t = num, digit ;

    while ( t != 0 )
    {
        digit = t % 10 ;
        sum = sum + factorial ( digit ) ;
        t = t / 10 ;
    }

    if ( sum == num )
        return true ;
    else
        return false ;
}
```

## Sample Run

List of curious numbers:
1
2
145

## Explanation

The **isCurious( )** function extracts each digit of the number passed to it and keeps a running sum of the factorial values of each digit. Lastly, it reports whether the number is a curious number or not. The **factorial( )** function is called for each digit of the number to obtain the factorial value of that digit.

## Challenge 10

The Fibonacci sequence is defined by the recurrence relation:

$F(n) = F(n-1) + F(n-2)$, where $F(1) = 1$ and $F(2) = 1$.

Hence the first 12 terms will be:

$F(1) = 1$
$F(2) = 1$
$F(3) = 2$
$F(4) = 3$
$F(5) = 5$
$F(6) = 8$
$F(7) = 13$
$F(8) = 21$
$F(9) = 34$
$F(10) = 55$
$F(11) = 89$
$F(12) = 144$

The 12th term, $F(12)$, is the first term to contain three digits.

Write a program to find the index of the first term in the Fibonacci sequence to contain 10 digits?

## Solution

```
// Project: chall10
// Program to find the first number and its index in the Fibonacci
// sequence that contains 10 digits
#include <iostream>
using namespace std ;
```

```
int countdigits ( int ) ;

int main( )
{
    int a = 1, b = 1, c ;
    int count, index = 3 ;

    while ( 1 )
    {
        c = a + b ;
        count = countdigits ( c ) ;
        if ( count == 10 )
        {
            cout << "Number = " << c << endl ;
            cout << "Index of " << c << " in the fibonacci sequence = "
                << index << endl ;
            break ;
        }
        index++ ;
        a = b ;
        b = c ;
    }
    return 0 ;
}

int countdigits ( int num )
{
    int count = 0 ;

    while ( num != 0 )
    {
        num = num / 10 ;
        count++ ;
    }
    return count ;
}
```

## Sample Run

Number = 1134903170

Index of 1134903170 in the fibonacci sequence = 45

## Explanation

In the infinite **while** loop a new term of Fibonacci sequence is calculated through the statement **c = a + b**. Then, by calling the **countDigits( )** function the number of digits in that term ( **c** ) is obtained. If this function returns 10, it means the current term of the Fibonacci sequence contains 10 digits. In that case, the term and its **index** is printed out. If not, **index** is incremented and **a** & **b** are reassigned, so that next term of the sequence can be calculated. The initial value of **index** is set to 3 because the first two terms are 1 and 1, and the **while** loop begins generating the terms from 3$^{rd}$ term onwards.

## Challenge 11

January 1$^{st}$ 1900 was a Monday. The months April, June, September and November have 30 days, whereas the rest have 31 days, except February which has 29 or 28 depending on whether the year is leap or not. A leap year occurs on any year evenly divisible by 4, but not on a century unless it is divisible by 400. Write a program to find out how many Sundays fell on the first of the month during the twentieth century (January 1$^{st}$ 1901 to December 31$^{st}$ 2000)?

## Solution

```
// Project: chall11
// Program that finds the number of Sundays that occurred on the first
// of a month during the 20th century.
// It is given that January 1st, 1900 was a Monday.

#include <iostream>
using namespace std ;

enum month
{
    JAN, FEB, MAR, APR, MAY, JUN, JUL, AUG, SEP, OCT, NOV, DEC
} ;
```

```
enum day
{
    MON, TUE, WED, THU, FRI, SAT, SUN
} ;

int numSundaysFirst( ) ;
bool isLeap ( int ) ;

int main( )
{
    int num ;

    num = numSundaysFirst( ) ;
    cout << "No. of Sundays on 1st of a month during 20th century = "
        << num << endl ;

    return 0 ;
}

int numSundaysFirst( )
{
    int firstday, sundaycount, lastday ;

    firstday = MON ;  // January 1st, 1900 is given to be a Monday

    // setting the last day of 1900, i.e. 31st December, 1900
    if ( isLeap ( 1900 ) )
        lastday = TUE ;
    else
        lastday = MON ;

    sundaycount = 0 ;
    for ( int year = 1901 ; year <= 2000 ; year++ )
    {
        for ( int month = JAN ; month <= DEC ; month++ )
        {
            firstday = ( lastday + 1 ) % 7 ;

            if ( firstday == SUN )
                sundaycount++ ;
```

```
switch ( month )
{
    case JAN :
    case MAR :
    case MAY :
    case JUL :
    case AUG :
    case OCT :
    case DEC :
        lastday = ( firstday + 2 ) % 7 ;
        break ;

    case APR :
    case JUN :
    case SEP :
    case NOV :
        lastday = ( firstday + 1 ) % 7 ;
        break ;

    case FEB :
        if ( isLeap ( year ) )
            lastday = firstday ;
        else
            lastday = ( firstday + 6 ) % 7 ;
        break ;
        }
    }
}

    return sundaycount ;
}

bool isLeap ( int year )
{
    if ( ( year % 100 != 0 ) && ( year % 4 == 0 ) || ( year % 400 == 0 ) )
        return true ;
    else
        return false ;
}
```

## Sample Run

The number of Sundays on 1st of a month during the 20th century = 171

## Explanation

Firstly a few facts:

The last day of a year is same as the first day of the year if the year is not leap, and 1 day from the first day if the year is leap. For example, if the first day of the year is a Monday, then the last day would be a Monday if the year is not leap and a Tuesday if the year is leap.

If a month contains 31 days, then the last day of the month is 2 days away from the first day of the month. For example, if $1^{st}$ January is a Tuesday, then $31^{st}$ January is a Thursday. If $1^{st}$ January is a Sunday, then $31^{st}$ January is a Tuesday.

If a month contains 30 days, then the last day of the month is 1 day away from the first day of the month. For example, if $1^{st}$ June is a Tuesday, then $30^{th}$ June is a Wednesday. Similarly, if $1^{st}$ June is a Sunday, then $30^{th}$ June is a Monday.

If February has 28 days, then the last day of February is 6 days away from the first day of the month. Also, if February has 29 days, then the last day is the same as the first day of the month.

As stated in the problem statement, $1^{st}$ January 1900 was a Monday. Firstly, we have checked whether 1900 is a leap year or not, and thereby determined the last day of the year 1900.

To ensure that the days rotate over from Sunday, while finding the last day of the month, we use the mod operation.

Through the **for** loops we have iterated over from 1901 to 2000, and then for each month within every year. Inside the loops we have checked what the first day of the month is, and if it is Sunday, we increment the count. Then find the last day of the month, and therefore the first day of the next month by using the facts stated above.

Lastly, we have displayed the count that is obtained.

## Challenge 12

Write a program that determines the number of trailing zeros at the end of X! (X factorial), where X is an arbitrary number that is input through the keyboard. For instance, 5! is 120, so it has one trailing zero.

## Solution

```
// Project: chall12
// Program to find the number of trailing zeros in factorial value
#include <iostream>
using namespace std ;

int main( )
{
    int n, i, k ;
    int count = 0 ;

    cout << "Enter a non-negative number: " << endl ;
    cin >> n ;

    if ( n >= 0 )
    {
        for ( i = 1 ; i <= n ; i++ )
        {
            k = i ;
            while ( k % 5 == 0 )
            {
                count++ ;
                k = k / 5 ;
            }
        }

        cout << "No. of zeros at the end of " << n << "! = "
            << count << endl ;
    }
    else
        cout << "Invalid Input" << endl ;
}
```

## Sample Runs

Enter a non-negative number:
12
No. of zeros at the end of 12! = 2

Enter a non-negative number:
5
No. of zeros at the end of 5! = 1

## Explanation

We could have written a straight-forward program to first calculate the Factorial value of the number entered using a recursive function shown below.

```
int factorial ( int num )
{
    int p ;

    if ( num != 0 )
        p = num * factorial ( num - 1 ) ;
    else
        return 1 ;

    return p ;
}
```

Once the factorial value is obtained we can pass it to a function **CountTrailingZeros( )** to count the trailing zeros in the factorial value by extracting digits from the end of the number and counting them if they are zeros. This approach has a serious limitation. The range of an **int** would be quickly exceeded while calculating the factorial value. So this approach would give wrong results beyond 13!. Hence we have used a different approach to count the trailing zeros.

In this approach we have just counted the number of times 5 occurs in the multiplications involved in the calculation of factorial value. This is enough because a trailing zero in a factorial value would come when 10 is a factor of the factorial value. And 10 is nothing but 5 x 2. So if we count number of 5s involved in the multiplications we would know how many trailing zeros are present in the factorial value.

Thus if number entered is 12 then 12! would be

1 x 2 x 3 x 4 x 5 x 6 x 7 x 8 x 9 x 10 x 11 x 12

Here there are 2 5s involved in the multiplications. The first 5 is obvious, the second 5 comes from 10, which is 5 x 2. Hence 12! would have 2 trailing 0s at the end.

## Challenge   13

A triplet of positive integers (a,b,c) is called a Cardano Triplet if it satisfies the condition:

$$\sqrt[3]{(a + b\sqrt{c})} + \sqrt[3]{(a - b\sqrt{c})} = 1$$

For example, (2,1,5) is a Cardano Triplet.

Write a progam to generate all Cardano Triplets that exist, such that ( a + b + c ) <= 100.

## Solution

```
// Project: chall13
// Program that generates Cardano triplets
#include <iostream>
#include <cmath>

using namespace std ;
bool isCardano ( int, int, int ) ;

int main( )
{
    int count = 0 ;

    for ( int a = 1 ; a <= 100 ; a++ )
    {
        for ( int b = 1 ; b <= 100 ; b++ )
```

```
        {
            for ( int c = 1 ; c <= 100 ; c++ )
            {
                if ( a + b + c <= 100 )
                {
                    if ( isCardano ( a, b, c ) )
                    {
                        count++ ;
                        cout << "Cardano Triplet " << count << ": "
                             << a << ", " << b << ", " << c << endl ;
                    }
                }
            }
        }
    }

    cout << "Total number of Cardano triplets = " << count << endl ;
    return 0 ;
}

bool isCardano ( int a, int b, int c )
{
    float brc = b * sqrt ( c ) ;
    float num = cbrt ( a + brc ) + cbrt ( a - brc ) ;

    if ( num < 1.000001 && num > 0.999999 )
        return true ;
    else
        return false ;
}
```

## Sample Run

```
Cardano Triplet 1: 2, 1, 5
Cardano Triplet 2: 5, 1, 52
Cardano Triplet 3: 5, 2, 13
Cardano Triplet 4: 8, 3, 21
Cardano Triplet 5: 11, 4, 29
Cardano Triplet 6: 14, 5, 37
Cardano Triplet 7: 17, 6, 45
Cardano Triplet 8: 17, 9, 20
```

Cardano Triplet 9: 17, 18, 5
Cardano Triplet 10: 20, 7, 53
Cardano Triplet 11: 23, 8, 61
Total number of Cardano triplets = 11

## Explanation

The program runs 3 **for** loops to give values to variables **a**, **b**, and **c** from 1 to 100. During each iteration **isCardano( )** is called. This function checks whether the condition for Cardano triplet is satisfied or not. Since the condition involves cube and square roots the sum of two terms might not turn out to be exactly 1. So we accept the triplet as Cardano triplet, if the sum is between 0.99999 and 1.000001.

## Challenge 14

Write a program to determine if the integers in an array follow either an arithmetic or geometric progression. An arithmetic progression is one where the difference between each successive pair of integers is constant, for example in the array [2, 4, 6, 8] the difference between the integers is always 2. A geometric progression is one where each element in the array is the product of the previous integer multiplied by some constant or ratio, for example in the array [3, 9, 27, 81] each element is a result of the previous element multiplied by 3.

## Solution

```
// Project: chall14
// Program to determine if a sequence is an AP or a GP or none
#include <iostream>
using namespace std ;

bool isAP ( int*, int ) ;
bool isGP ( int*, int ) ;

const int MAX = 5 ;

int main( )
```

```
{
    int arr[ MAX ] ;
    bool ap, gp ;

    cout << "Enter " << MAX << " terms of the sequence: " << endl ;
    for ( int i = 0 ; i < MAX ; i++ )
        cin >> arr[ i ] ;

    ap = isAP ( arr, MAX ) ;

    if ( ap == true )
        cout << "The sequence is an AP" << endl ;
    else
        cout << "The sequence is not an AP" << endl ;

    gp = isGP ( arr, MAX ) ;

    if ( gp == true )
        cout << "The sequence is a GP" << endl ;
    else
        cout << "The sequence is not a GP" << endl ;

    return 0 ;
}

bool isAP ( int* arr, int size )
{
    int diff ;
    bool ap = true ;

    diff = arr[ 1 ] - arr[ 0 ] ;

    for ( int i = 2 ; i < size ; i++ )
    {
        int t = arr[ i ] - arr[ i - 1 ] ;
        if ( t != diff )
        {
            ap = false ;
            break ;
        }
    }
```

```cpp
        return ap ;
}

bool isGP ( int* arr, int size )
{
    float ratio ;
    bool gp = true ;

    for ( int i = 0 ; i < size ; i++ )
    {
        if ( arr[ i ] == 0 )
        {
            gp = false ;
            break ;
        }
    }

    if ( gp == true )
    {
        ratio = ( float ) arr[ 1 ] / ( float ) arr[ 0 ] ;

        for ( int i = 2 ; i < size ; i++ )
        {
            float t = ( float ) arr[ i ] / ( float ) arr[ i - 1 ] ;
            if ( t != ratio )
            {
                gp = false ;
                break ;
            }
        }
    }

    return gp ;
}
```

## Sample Runs

Enter 5 terms of the sequence:
5 10 15 20 25
The sequence is an AP.

The sequence is not a GP.

Enter 5 terms of the sequence:
1 3 5 7 9
The sequence is an AP
The sequence is not a GP

## Explanation

The program receives 5 elements of an integer array and then calls **isAP( )** and **isGP( )** to determine whether the numbers are in arithmetic or geometric progression. In **isGP( )** firstly it is checked whether any term in the sequence is 0. If so, then false is returned because in that case terms cannot be in geometric progression.

# 03 / Total Challenges: 7

# Basic C++ Challenges

There are many new non-OOP (Object Oriented Programming) features introduced in C++. These features make writing programs easy and efficient. This chapter poses challenges related to these features.

## Challenge 15

Write a program that receives from keyboard and outputs on screen the primitives like char, short integer, long integer, float, double, long double and string using scanf( ) / printf( ) as well as cin / cout.

## Solution

```
// Project: chall15
// C, C++ style Input/Output
#include <iostream>
#include <cstdio>
using namespace std ;

int main( )
{
    // C Style
    char ch ;
    int n ;
    long int num ;
    float f ;
    double d ;
    long double ld ;

    printf ( "Enter a character: \n" ) ;
    scanf ( "%c", &ch ) ;

    printf ( "Enter an integer: \n" ) ;
    scanf ( "%d", &n ) ;

    printf ( "Enter a long integer: \n" ) ;
    scanf ( "%ld", &num ) ;

    printf ( "Enter a float: \n" ) ;
    scanf ( "%f", &f ) ;

    printf ( "Enter a double: \n" ) ;
    scanf ( "%lf", &d ) ;
```

```
printf ( "Enter a long double: \n" ) ;
scanf ( "%Lf", &ld ) ;

printf ( "Character: %c\n", ch ) ;
printf ( "Integer: %d\n", n ) ;
printf ( "Long Integer: %ld\n", num ) ;
printf ( "Float: %f\n", f ) ;
printf ( "Double: %lf\n", d ) ;
printf ( "Long Double: %Lf\n\n", ld ) ;

// C++ Style
char cpp_ch ;
int cpp_n ;
long int cpp_num ;
float cpp_f ;
double cpp_d ;
long double cpp_ld ;

cout << "Enter a character: " << endl ;
cin >> cpp_ch ;

cout << "Enter an integer: " << endl ;
cin >> cpp_n ;

cout << "Enter a long integer: " << endl ;
cin >> cpp_num ;

cout << "Enter a float: " << endl ;
cin >> cpp_f ;

cout << "Enter a double: " << endl ;
cin >> cpp_d ;

cout << "Enter a long double: " << endl ;
cin >> cpp_ld ;

cout << "Character: " << cpp_ch << endl ;
cout << "Integer: " << cpp_n << endl ;
cout << "Long Integer: " << cpp_num << endl ;
cout << "Float: " << cpp_f << endl ;
cout << "Double: " << cpp_d << endl ;
```

```
    cout << "Long Double: " << cpp_ld << endl ;

    return 0 ;
}
```

## Sample Run

```
Enter a character:
A
Enter an integer:
23
Enter a long integer:
3650000
Enter a float:
3.14
Enter a double:
6.28
Enter a long double:
3.141414
Character: A
Integer: 23
Long Integer: 3650000
Float: 3.140000
Double: 6.280000
Long Double: 3.141414

Enter a character:
D
Enter an integer:
44
Enter a long integer:
454545
Enter a float:
4.44
Enter a double:
55555.5555
Enter a long double:
343434.343434
Character: D
Integer: 44
Long Integer: 454545
```

Float: 4.44
Double: 55555.6
Long Double: 343434

## Explanation

The program shows how to receive different data types and output them. To do so C uses functions **scanf( )** and **printf( )**, whereas C++ uses objects **cin** and **cout**. Objects are like variables. These objects are predefined for us in file "iostream". **cout** is an object of type **ostream,** whereas **cin** is an object of the type **istream. ostream** and **istream** are pre-defined types.

## Challenge 16

Write a program that makes it easy to change the size of the array and the associated code to process the array in C style as well as C++ style.

## Solution

```
// Project: chall16
// C, C++ array size changes
#include <iostream>
#include <cstdio>
using namespace std ;

#define MAX 5

int main( )
{
    // C Style
    int arr[ MAX ], i ;
    for ( i = 0 ; i < MAX ; i++ )
    {
        printf ( "Enter element of the array: " ) ;
        scanf ( "%d", &arr[i] ) ;
    }
```

```
printf ( "Array Elements: " ) ;
for ( i = 0 ; i < MAX ; i++ )
    printf ( "%d\t", arr[i] ) ;
printf ( "\n\n" ) ;

// C++ Style
const int size = 5 ;
int cppArr[ size ] ;

for ( int i = 0 ; i < size ; i++ )
{
    cout << "Enter element of the array: " ;
    cin >> cppArr[i] ;
}

cout << "Array Elements: " ;
for ( int i = 0 ; i < size ; i++ )
    cout << cppArr[i] << "\t" ;
cout << endl ;

return 0 ;
}
```

## Sample Run

```
Enter element of the array: 12
Enter element of the array: 23
Enter element of the array: 33
Enter element of the array: 22
Enter element of the array: 65
Array Elements: 12    23    33    22    65

Enter element of the array: 33
Enter element of the array: 55
Enter element of the array: 77
Enter element of the array: 88
Enter element of the array: 99
Array Elements: 33    55    77    88    99
```

## Explanation

**#define** has a global scope. It means its effect would be throughout the file. As against this, **const** can have a local or a global scope depending upon where it is defined.

Here **MAX** has a global scope, whereas **size** has a local scope since it is defined in **main( )**. We cannot use **size** in other functions. If we want it to have a global scope then we have to define it outside **main( )**.

Using **const int** is a better idea than using **#define**, since we can control its scope.

## Challenge  17

Write a program that receives the size of an array and then allocates memory for it dynamically. Further, receive numbers into this array and print them on screen. The program should use C and C++ styles to accomplish these tasks.

## Solution

```
// Project: chall17
// C, C++ style dynamic memory allocation
#include <iostream>
#include <cstdio>
#include <cstdlib>
using namespace std ;

int main( )
{
    // C Style
    int size ;
    printf ( "Enter size of the array: \n" ) ;
    scanf ( "%d", &size ) ;

    if ( size > 0 )
    {
```

```
    int *arr, *p, i ;
    arr = ( int* ) malloc ( sizeof ( int ) * size ) ;
    p = arr ;

    for ( i = 0 ; i < size ; i++ )
    {
        printf ( "Enter array element: \n" ) ;
        scanf ( "%d", p ) ;
        p++ ;
    }
    p = arr ;

    printf ( "Array Elements: \n" ) ;
    for ( i = 0 ; i < size ; i++ )
    {
        printf ( "%d\t", *p ) ;
        p++ ;
    }
    free ( arr ) ;
}
else
    printf ( "Invalid Input: Array size must be a +ve integer\n" ) ;

// C++ Style
int cppSize ;
cout << endl << "Enter size of the array: " << endl ;
cin >> cppSize ;

if ( cppSize > 0 )
{
    int *cppArr, *cppP ;
    cppArr = new int[ cppSize ] ;
    cppP = cppArr ;

    for ( int i = 0 ; i < cppSize ; i++ )
    {
        cout << "Enter array element: " << endl ;
        cin >> *cppP ;
        cppP++ ;
    }
```

```
        cppP = cppArr ;

        cout << "Array Elements: " << endl ;
        for ( int i = 0 ; i < cppSize ; i++ )
        {
            cout << *cppP << "\t" ;
            cppP++ ;
        }
        delete [ ] cppArr ;
    }
    else
        cout << "Invalid Input: Array size must be a +ve integer" << endl ;

    return 0 ;
}
```

## Sample Run

```
Enter size of the array:
6
Enter array element:
12
Enter array element:
23
Enter array element:
34
Enter array element:
45
Enter array element:
56
Enter array element:
67
Array Elements:
12    23    34    45    56    67
Enter size of the array:
6
Enter array element:
10
Enter array element:
20
Enter array element:
```

```
30
Enter array element:
40
Enter array element:
50
Enter array element:
60
Array Elements:
10    20    30    40    50    60
```

## Explanation

Compare the following memory allocation styles:

arr = ( int* ) malloc ( sizeof ( int ) * size ) ;
cppArr = new int[ cppSize ] ;

**malloc( )** is a standard library function in C that helps us allocate a chunk of bytes. It returns the base address of the chunk as a **void \***, so we need to cast it appropriately. In this case we have casted it into an **int \*** since we wish to use that allocated chunk as an integer array.

In C++, the same task is achieved using the **new** operator. There is no need to do typecasting while using **new**, since it returns a pointer of the appropriate type.

In both cases, memory for the array is allocated for the array dynamically, i.e. during program execution. As a result, we can receive the size of the array during execution and then allocate space for an array of that size. This gives us flexibility of altering the array size during every execution without making any changes in the program.

## Challenge 18

Write a program that receives two numbers from keyboard and then swaps them using a call by address and a call by reference.

## Solution

```cpp
// Project: chall18
// Swap by address and reference
#include <iostream>
using namespace std ;

void swapByAddress ( int*, int* ) ;
void swapByReference ( int&, int& ) ;

int main( )
{
    int a, b ;

    cout << "Enter two numbers: " << endl ;
    cin >> a >> b ;

    swapByAddress ( &a, &b ) ;

    cout << "After swapping numbers by address: " << endl ;
    cout << "a: " << a << " b: " << b << endl ;

    swapByReference ( a, b ) ;

    cout << "After swapping numbers by reference: " << endl ;
    cout << "a: " << a << " b: " << b << endl ;

    return 0 ;
}

void swapByAddress ( int *addrA, int *addrB )
{
    int t ;

    t = *addrA ;
    *addrA = *addrB ;
    *addrB = t ;
}

void swapByReference ( int &refA, int &refB )
```

```
{
    int t ;

    t = refA ;
    refA = refB ;
    refB = t ;
}
```

## Sample Run

Enter two numbers:
10 20
After swapping numbers by address:
a: 20 b: 10
After swapping numbers by reference:
a: 10 b: 20

## Explanation

In **swapByAddress( )**, using pointers we are able to change the values of **a** and **b** of **main( )**. The same is also achieved using references in **swapByReference( )**.

A reference is nothing but a constant pointer that gets automatically dereferenced. This means **refA** and **refB** are constant pointers to **a** and **b**. Also, when we use **refA** and **refB** what gets used is **\*refA** and **\*refB**. This is automatic dereferencing.

## Challenge   19

Write a program that implements multiple versions of **abso( )** function to find absolute value of **int**, **float**, **long int**, **double** and **long double**.

## Solution

```
// Project: chall19
// C++ Function Overloading
#include <iostream>
```

```cpp
using namespace std ;

int abso ( int ) ;
long int abso ( long int ) ;
float abso ( float ) ;
double abso ( double ) ;
long double abso ( long double ) ;

int main( )
{
    int n ;
    long int num ;
    float f ;
    double d ;
    long double ld ;

    cout << "Enter an integer: " << endl ;
    cin >> n ;

    n = abso ( n ) ;
    cout << "Absolute value of integer: " << n << endl ;

    cout << "Enter a long integer: " << endl ;
    cin >> num ;

    num = abs ( num ) ;
    cout << "Absolute value of long integer: " << num << endl ;

    cout << "Enter a float: " << endl ;
    cin >> f ;

    f = abso ( f ) ;
    cout << "Absolute value of float: " << f << endl ;

    cout << "Enter a double: " << endl ;
    cin >> d ;

    d = abso ( d ) ;
    cout << "Absolute value of double: " << d << endl ;

    cout << "Enter a long double: " << endl ;
```

```
    cin >> ld ;

    ld = abso ( ld ) ;
    cout << "Absolute value of long double: " << ld << endl ;

    return 0 ;
}

int abso ( int n )
{
    if ( n < 0 )
        return -1 * n ;
    else
        return n ;
}

long int abso ( long int num )
{
    if ( num < 0 )
        return -1 * num ;
    else
        return num ;
}

float abso ( float f )
{
    if ( f < 0 )
        return -1 * f ;
    else
        return f ;
}

double abso ( double d )
{
    if ( d < 0 )
        return -1 * d ;
    else
        return d ;
}

long double abso ( long double ld )
```

```
{
    if ( ld < 0 )
        return -1 * ld ;
    else
        return ld ;
}
```

## Sample Run

Enter an integer:
-34
Absolute value of integer: 34
Enter a long integer:
45678
Absolute value of long integer: 45678
Enter a float:
-3.14
Absolute value of float: 3.14
Enter a double:
4567.88
Absolute value of double: 4567.88
Enter a long double:
-12345.6
Absolute value of long double: 12345.6

## Explanation

In C++ we can give same names to different function so long as they differ in number, order or type of arguments. Hence, we could define several versions of the **abso( )** function here. This feature of C++ is known as Function Overloading. The advantage of this feature is that we do not have to remember names of different functions which are essentially carrying out similar jobs. So, there is no need for defining and remembering functions like **iabso( )**, **fabso( )**, **dabso( )**, etc.

## Challenge 20

Write a program that defines a function that receives 5 arguments—**char**, **int**, **long**, **float** and **double** in that order. Make 3 calls to this function. In the second call pass only 4 arguments; the last one should be taken as 6.28 by default. In the third call pass only 3 arguments. In this case the fourth argument should be taken as 3.14 and fifth as 6.28 by default.

### Solution

```
// Project: chall20
// Default values for arguments
#include <iostream>
using namespace std ;

void fun ( char, int, long int, float = 3.14, double = 6.28 ) ;

int main( )
{
    fun ( 'A', 12, 123, 0.5, -1.5 ) ;
    fun ( 'B', 1234, 12345, 4.5 ) ;
    fun ( 'C', 987, 9876 ) ;

    return 0 ;
}

void fun ( char ch, int n, long int num, float f, double d )
{
    cout << ch << "\t" << n << "\t" << num << "\t" << f << "\t" << d
        << endl ;
}
```

### Sample Run

```
A    12    123    0.5    -1.5
B    1234  12345  4.5    6.28
C    987   9876   3.14   6.28
```

## Explanation

Look at the prototype of **fun( )**. It shows default values for fourth and fifth arguments. In the first call to **fun( )** since we have passed all 5 arguments, the default values are ignored. In the second call to **fun( )**, we have passed only the first 4 arguments, the fifth takes the default value 6.28. Lastly, in the third call to **fun( )**, we have passed only 3 arguments, the fourth and fifth take the default values mentioned in the prototype.

## Challenge  21

Write a program that has a function **findmax( )** that receives variable number of arguments and finds and returns the maximum out of them.

## Solution

```
// Project: chall21
// Function receiving variable number of arguments
#include <iostream>
#include <cstdarg>

using namespace std ;

int findmax ( int, ...) ;
int main( )
{
    int  max ;

    max = findmax ( 5, 23, 15, 1, 92, 50 ) ;
    cout << "maximum = " << max << endl ;
    max = findmax ( 3, 100, 300, 29 ) ;
    cout << "maximum = " << max << endl ;
    return 0 ;
}

int findmax ( int count, ... )
{
```

```
int  max, i, num ;

va_list  ptr ;

va_start ( ptr, count ) ;
max = va_arg ( ptr, int ) ;

for ( i = 1 ; i < count ; i++ )
{
    num = va_arg ( ptr, int ) ;
    if ( num > max )
        max = num ;
}

return ( max ) ;
}
```

## Sample Run

```
A    12    123    0.5    -1.5
B    1234  12345  4.5    6.28
C    987   9876   3.14   6.28
```

## Explanation

Look at the prototype of **findmax( )**. The ellipses **( ... )** indicate that the number of arguments after the first argument would be variable.

Observe the two calls to **findmax( )**. In the first call we have passed 6 arguments to it, whereas in the second we have passed 4 arguments to it. There are three macros available in the file "**stdarg.h**" called **va_start**, **va_arg** and **va_list**, which allow us to handle this situation. These macros provide a method for accessing the arguments of the function when a function takes a fixed number of arguments followed by a variable number of arguments. The fixed number of arguments are accessed in the normal way, whereas the optional arguments are accessed using the macros **va_start** and **va_arg**. Out of these macros, **va_start** is used to initialize a pointer to the beginning of the list of optional arguments. On the other hand, the macro **va_arg** is used to advance the pointer to the next argument.

Here we are making two calls to **findmax( )**, first time to find maximum out of 5 values and second time to find maximum out of 3 values. Note that for each call the first argument is the count of arguments that follow the first argument. The value of the first argument passed to **findmax( )** is collected in the variable **count**. **findmax( )** begins with a declaration of a pointer **ptr** of the type **va_list**. Observe the next statement carefully.

va_start ( ptr, tot_num ) ;

This statement sets up **ptr** such that it points to the first variable argument in the list. If we are considering the first call to **findmax( )**, **ptr** would now point to 23. The statement **max = va_arg ( ptr, int )** would assign the integer being pointed to by **ptr** to **max**. Thus 23 would be assigned to **max**, and **ptr** would now start pointing to the next argument, i.e., 15. The rest of the program is fairly straightforward. We just keep picking up successive numbers in the list and keep comparing them with the latest value in **max**, till all the arguments in the list have been scanned. The final value in **max** is then returned to **main( )**.

# 04 / Total Challenges: 7

# Class Organization Challenges

There is a lot of flexibility when it comes to organizing classes. This flexibility ensures that we can decide whom to provide access to source code of the class. If we organize classes in libraries then the user of the class would have access only to the class declaration, whereas its implementation would remain hidden from the user of the class. This chapter checks your understanding about class organization and its related issues.

## Challenge  22

Write a self-sufficient class called **Number** which maintains an **int**. It should have following methods in it to perform various operation on the **int**:

void setNumber ( int n ) ; // sets n into int

int getNumber( ) ; // return current value of int

void printNumber( ) ; // prints the int

bool isNegative( ) ; // checks whether int is negative

bool isDivisibleBy ( int n ) ; // checks whether int is divisible by n

int absoluteValue( ) ; // returns absolute value of int

## Solution

```
// Project: chall22
// Self-sufficient number class
#include <stdio.h>
#include <iostream>
using namespace std ;

class Number
{
    private :
        int num ;

    public :
        void setNumber ( int n )
        {
            num = n ;
        }

        int getNumber( )
        {
            return num ;
        }
```

```
void printNumber( )
{
    cout << num << endl ;
}

bool isNegative( )
{
    if ( num < 0 )
        return true ;
    else
        return false ;
}

bool isDivisibleBy ( int n )
{
    if ( n == 0 )
        return false ;
    else
    {
        if ( num % n == 0 )
            return true ;
        else
            return false ;
    }
}

int absoluteValue( )
{
    if ( num >= 0 )
        return num ;
    else
        return -1 * num ;
}
};

int main( )
{
    Number x ;

    x.setNumber ( 1234 ) ;
```

```
    x.printNumber( ) ;

    if ( x.isDivisibleBy ( 5 ) == true )
        cout << "5 divides " << x.getNumber( ) << endl ;
    else
        cout << "5 does not divide " << x.getNumber( ) << endl ;

    cout << "Absolute Value of " << x.getNumber( ) << " is "
            << x.absoluteValue( ) << endl ;
}
```

## Sample Run

```
1234
5 does not divide 1234
Absolute Value of 1234 is 1234
```

## Explanation

A self-sufficient class means all its members are defined within the class. Here, the data members and member functions of **Number** are defined right inside the class.

Such an organization of the class is no doubt workable, but suffers from an important limitation. If we are to give this class to some other person then he gets an access to complete source code of the class. This is not desirable, especially when you are developing a class library for others to use.

## Challenge  23

Rewrite the program in Challenge 22 with all member functions defined outside the **Number** class.

## Solution

```
// Project: chall23
// Number class with functions defined outside the class
```

```cpp
#include <iostream>
using namespace std ;

class Number
{
    private :
        int num ;
    public :
        void setNumber ( int ) ;
        int getNumber( ) ;
        void printNumber( ) ;
        bool isNegative( ) ;
        bool isDivisibleBy ( int n ) ;
        int absoluteValue( ) ;
} ;

void Number :: setNumber ( int n )
{
    num = n ;
}

int Number :: getNumber( )
{
    return num ;
}

void Number :: printNumber( )
{
    cout << num << endl ;
}

bool Number :: isNegative( )
{
    if ( num < 0 )
        return true ;
    else
        return false ;
}

bool Number :: isDivisibleBy ( int n )
{
```

```cpp
    if ( n == 0 )
        return false ;
    else
    {
        if ( num % n == 0 )
            return true ;
        else
            return false ;
    }
}

int Number :: absoluteValue( )
{
    if ( num >= 0 )
        return num ;
    else
        return -1 * num ;
}

int main( )
{
    Number x ;

    x.setNumber ( 1234 ) ;
    x.printNumber( ) ;

    if ( x.isDivisibleBy ( 5 ) == true )
        cout << "5 divides " << x.getNumber( ) << endl ;
    else
        cout << "5 does not divide " << x.getNumber( ) << endl ;

    cout << "Absolute Value of: " << x.getNumber( ) << " is "
            << x.absoluteValue( ) << endl ;
}
```

## Sample Run

```
1234
5 does not divide 1234
Absolute Value of 1234 is 1234
```

## Explanation

This program presents another way of organizing the **Number** class. The advantage of this organization is that since the class merely contains data members and member functions declarations, the class declaration becomes very compact. As a result, it is very easy to understand what the class is really up to. An easy understanding of the class goes a long way in its optimal usage.

## Challenge 24

Rewrite program in Challenge 22 with class declaration in "Number.h" file, class declaration in "Number.cpp" file. Use this class from "main.cpp" file.

## Solution

```cpp
// Project: chall24
// Number.h - contains class declaration
#ifndef NUMBER_H
#define NUMBER_H
class Number
{
    private :
        int num ;
    public:
        void setNumber ( int ) ;
        int getNumber( ) ;
        void printNumber( ) ;
        bool isNegative( ) ;
        bool isDivisibleBy ( int ) ;
        int absoluteValue( ) ;
} ;
#endif

// Number.cpp - contains definitions of member functions of Number
// class
#include "Number.h"
```

```cpp
#include <iostream>
using namespace std ;

void Number :: setNumber ( int n )
{
    num = n ;
}

int Number :: getNumber( )
{
    return num ;
}

void Number :: printNumber( )
{
    cout << num << endl ;
}

bool Number :: isNegative( )
{
    if ( num < 0 )
        return true ;
    else
        return false ;
}

bool Number :: isDivisibleBy ( int n )
{
    if ( n == 0 )
        return false ;
    else
    {
        if ( num % n == 0 )
            return true ;
        else
            return false ;
    }
}

int Number :: absoluteValue( )
{
```

```
        if ( num >= 0 )
            return num ;
        else
            return -1 * num ;
}

// main.cpp - contains code that uses the Number class
#include <iostream>
#include "Number.h"
using namespace std ;

int main( )
{
    Number x ;
    x.setNumber ( 1234 ) ;
    x.printNumber( );

    if ( x.isDivisibleBy ( 5 ) == true )
        cout << "5 divides " << x.getNumber( ) << endl ;
    else
        cout << "5 does not divide " << x.getNumber( ) << endl ;

    cout << "Absolute value of " << x.getNumber( ) << " is "
            << x.absoluteValue( ) << endl ;
    return 0 ;
}
```

## Sample Run

```
1234
5 does not divide 1234
Absolute Value of 1234 is 1234
```

## Explanation

This program presents another way of organizing the **Number** class. This program is loosely coupled in the sense that once all the members of the class have been declared in the class, different team members can be assigned the job of defining individual functions in different .cpp files. These files can later be #included in the file that contains **main( )**, in which objects of **Number** class are created and its member functions are called.

If you are using NetBeans to create this program, then first create a project by name 'chall24' and in its 'main.cpp' define **main( )**. Then right click on the project and select 'New | C++ class'. Give the class name as **Number**. As a result two files—'Number.h' and 'Number.cpp'—would get created in a new folder called 'Number'.

Before compilation one configuration change needs to be done. For this Right click on 'chall24' in the project window and select 'Properties' from the menu that pops up. On selection a 'Project Properties' dialog would appear. In this dialog choose 'C++ Compiler | Include Directories' and add 'Number' directory. This would ensure that when we include "Number.h" in 'main.cpp' and 'Number.cpp', it would be searched in the 'Number' directory.

If you are to compile the program using the command-line then do the following:

```
$ g++ -c main.cpp Number.cpp
```

## Challenge 25

What are Class Libraries? What are the different ways to organize them?

## Explanation

Class libraries are related classes compiled into object code. For example, the classes like **ostream**, **istream**, etc. that have been compiled into the C++ standard library. Many third-party class libraries are also available for purchase. For example, class library for fingerprint recognition, class library for 3D animation, class library for text to speech conversion, etc. Even we can create libraries out of our classes.

Class libraries can be of two types—statically linked or dynamically linked. Statically linked libraries become part of the executable code that uses the library. So, if there are three programs that use a statically-linked class library, the class library would become part of all three executables. This is not a good idea. This is because, if all three executables are executed then three copies of the same library would be present in memory.

As against this, if three executables use a dynamically-linked library then the library is loaded in memory only when the first executable is loaded. When the three executables are running all three would share one single copy of the library.

The statically-linked libraries have a '.LIB' extension under Windows and a '.a' extension under Linux. The dynamically-linked libraries have a '.dll' extension in both the environments.

## Challenge 26

Rewrite program in Challenge 22 such that **Number** class is stored in a Static Library.

## Solution

```
// Project - chall26
// main.cpp - contains code that uses the Number class
#include <iostream>
#include "Number.h"
using namespace std ;

int main( )
{
    ...
    // same code as in Challenge 24
}


// Project - NumberStaticLib
// Number.h - contains class declaration
#ifndef NUMBER_H
#define NUMBER_H
class Number
{
    // same code as in Challenge 24
    ...
```

```
} ;
#endif

// Project - NumberStaticLib
// Number.cpp - contains definitions of member functions of Number
// class
#include "Number.h"
#include <iostream>
using namespace std ;

void Number :: setNumber ( int n )
{
    num = n ;
}
...
// Same code as in Challenge 24
```

## Sample Run

```
1234
5 does not divide 1234
Absolute Value of 1234 is 1234
```

## Explanation

If you are using NetBeans first create a 'C++ Static Library' project by name 'NumberStaticLib'. Then right click on the project and select 'New | C++ class'. Name the class as **Number**. As a result two files— 'Number.h' and 'Number.cpp'—would get created in your project folder.

Add the **Number** class declaration in the 'Number.h' file and definition of **Number** class member functions in 'Number.cpp' file. Since we are using the file 'iostream' in this static library project we need to add its path in project configuration. For this, Right click on 'NumberStaticLib' in the project window and select 'Properties' from the menu that pops up. On selection a 'Project Properties' dialog would appear. In this dialog choose 'C++ Compiler | Include Directories' and add 'C:\cygwin\lib\gcc\i686-pc-cygwin\5.4.0\include\c++\' directory. This is where the 'iostream' file is present in a Cygwin g++ installation.

Build the program as usual using F6. This would create a static library file 'libnumberstaticlib.a' in the 'NumberStaticLib\dist\Debug\Cygwin-Windows' folder.

Next create a 'C++ Application' project called 'chall26' and in its main.cpp define **main( )** which uses the **Number** class. Copy the files 'libnumberstaticlib.a' and 'Number.h' into the 'chall26' project folder.

Right click on 'chall26' in the project window and select 'Properties' from the menu that pops up. On selection a 'Project Properties' dialog would appear. In this dialog choose 'Linker | Libraries | ...'. It would show the static library that we copied, namely 'libnumberstaticlib.a'. Select this file as the library file to link. Build the project using F6 and now 'chall26' would be able to use the static library.

If you wish to build the project using the command-line, carry out the following steps:

Build the 'NumberStaticLib' project using the command

$g++ -c Number.cpp –o libnumberstaticlib.a

Copy the files 'libnumberstaticlib.a' and 'Number.h' into the 'chall26' project folder.

Build the 'chall26' project using

$g++ main.cpp -I . -L . –llibnumberstaticlib -o chall26.exe

This would have created the executable 'chall26.exe' file. Execute it using

$ ./chall26.exe

## Challenge 27

Rewrite program in Challenge 22 such that **Number** class is stored in a Dynamically Linked Library.

## Solution

```
// Project - chall27
// main.cpp - contains code that uses the Number class
```

```
#include <iostream>
#include "Number.h"
using namespace std ;

int main( )
{
    ...
    // same code as in Challenge 24
}

// Project - NumberDynamicLib
// Number.h - contains class declaration
#ifndef NUMBER_H
#define NUMBER_H
class Number
{
    // same code as in Challenge 24
    ...
} ;
#endif

// Project - NumberDynamicLib
// Number.cpp - contains definitions of member functions of Number
// class
#include "Number.h"
#include <iostream>
using namespace std ;

void Number :: setNumber ( int n )
{
    num = n ;
}
...
// Same code as in Challenge 24
```

## Sample Run

```
1234
5 does not divide 1234
Absolute Value of 1234 is 1234
```

## Explanation

If you are using NetBeans first create a C++ Dynamic Library' project by name 'NumberDynamicLib'. Then right click on the project and select 'New | C++ class'. Name the class as **Number**. As a result two files—'Number.h' and 'Number.cpp'—would get created in your project folder.

Add the **Number** class declaration in the 'Number.h' file and definition of **Number** class member functions in 'Number.cpp' file. Since we are using the file 'iostream' in this dynamic library project we need to add its path in project configuration. For this, Right click on 'NumberDynamicLib' in the project window and select 'Properties' from the menu that pops up. On selection a 'Project Properties' dialog would appear. In this dialog choose 'C++ Compiler | Include Directories' and add 'C:\cygwin\lib\gcc\i686-pc-cygwin\5.4.0\include\c++\' directory. This is where the 'iostream' file is present in a Cygwin g++ installation.

Build the program as usual using F6. This would create a dynamically linkable library file. Its name would be 'libNumberDynamicLib.dll' and it would be present in the folder 'NumberDynamicLib\dist\Debug\Cygwin-Windows'.

Next create a 'C++ Application' project called 'chall27' and in its main.cpp define **main( )** which uses the **Number** class. Copy the files 'libNumberDynamicLib.dll' and 'Number.h' into the 'chall27' project folder.

Right click on 'chall27' in the project window and select 'Properties' from the menu that pops up. On selection a 'Project Properties' dialog would appear. In this dialog choose 'Linker | Libraries | ...'. It would show the dynamic library that we copied, namely 'libNumberDynamicLib.dll'. Select this file as the library file to link. Build the project using F6 and now 'chall27' would be able to use the dynamic library.

If you wish to build the project at command-line, carry out the following steps:

Build the NumberDynamicLib project using the command

$g++ -c Number.cpp –o libNumberDynamicLib.dll

Copy the files 'libNumberDynamicLib.dll' and 'Number.h' into the 'chall27' project folder.

Build the 'chall27' project using

$g++ main.cpp -I . -L . –llibNumberDynamicLib -shared -o chall27.exe

This would have created the executable chall26.exe file. Execute it using

$ ./chall27.exe

## Challenge 28

What is code portability? Are C++ programs created in Visual Studio portable? If not, how would you rectify that?

## Solution

Code portability means a given C++ program once compiled should work under all environments. For example a C++ program compiled under Windows environment should work under Linux too. But this does not happen, since the layout of the executable code under Windows is different than the layout under Linux. To be more specific Windows executables use a Portable Executable (PE) file format, whereas Linux executables use Executable and Linkable Format (ELF).

Thus, in C++ code portability cannot be achieved at executable code level. Can it be achieved at source code level? Means can a program created in Visual Studio be compiled using the g++ compile?

The C++ programs created using Visual Studio are non-portable if they use the file that the wizard includes in a C++ project by default—stdafx.h. Such programs would not be compiled using other compilers like g++.

For example, when you use Visual Studio to create a 'Win32 Console Application' the wizard creates the following code for you:

```
#include "stdafx.h"
int _tmain ( int argc, _TCHAR* argv[ ] )
{
    return 0 ;
}
```

You can delete this code and type your normal C++ program in its place. If you now compile the program using Ctrl F5 you would get the following error:

Fatal error C1010:
unexpected end of file while looking for precompiled header.
Did you forget to add '#include "stdafx.h"' to your source?

If you add #include "stdafx.h" at the top of your program then it would compile and run successfully. However, including this file makes the program Visual Studio-centric and would not get compiled with other C++ compilers. This is not good as the program no longer remains portable. To eliminate this error, you need to do a setting in Visual Studio by carrying out the following steps:

(a)  Go to 'Solution Explorer' window in your project.

(b)  Right click on the project name and select 'Properties' from the menu that pops up. On doing so, a dialog shown in Figure 4.1 would appear.

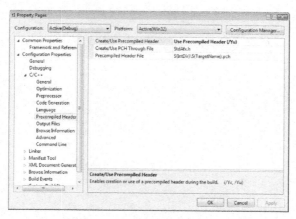

Figure 4.1

(c)  From the left pane of this dialog first select 'Configuration Properties' followed by 'C/C++'.

(d)  Select 'Precompiled Headers'

(e)  From the right pane of the dialog click on 'Create/Use Precompiled Header'. On doing so in the value for this option a triangle would appear.

(f)  Click on this triangle and a drop down list box would appear.

(g)  From the list box select 'Not using Precompiled Header'.

(h)  Click on OK button to make the setting effective.

After completing this setting the program would build successfully using Ctrl F5.

# 05 / Total Challenges: 9

# Class Constructor Challenges

**C**onstructor of a class gets called every time we create an object of that class. There are many types of constructors and hence many nuances involved while creating and using them. 9 Challenges in this chapter would test your understanding of all the details involved with creation of objects.

## Challenge 29

Which constructor is the default constructor? What does its body contain?

## Solution

```
// Project: hcall29
// Program to illustrate working of default constructor
#include <iostream>
using namespace std ;

class Sample
{
} ;

class Trial
{
    public :
        Trial( )
        {
            cout << "Trial's zero-argument constructor" ;
        }
} ;

int main( )
{
    Sample s ;
    Trial t ;

    return 0 ;
}
```

## Sample Run

Trial's zero-argument constructor

## Explanation

A default constructor is the zero-argument constructor in a class. It is called "default" constructor because if we do not provide it then the compiler would insert a public zero-argument constructor in our class.

Here the **Sample** class has no constructor; hence, the compiler would insert a zero-argument constructor in it. Had the compiler not done this, we would not have been able to create the object **s**. In the **Trial** class we have defined the zero-argument constructor; hence the compiler would not provide one.

## Challenge 30

Does the constructor actually "construct" an object? Can this be proven?

## Solution

```
// Project: hcall30
// Program to illustrate construction of object
#include <iostream>
using namespace std ;

class Sample
{
    public :

        Sample( )
        {
            cout << "Address of object passed to this function = "
                    << this << endl ;
        }
} ;

int main( )
{
    Sample s ;
```

```
    cout << "Address of object s = " << &s << endl ;

    return 0 ;
}
```

## Sample Run

Address of object passed to this function = 0x22cc7f
Address of object s = 0x22cc7f

## Explanation

Constructor doesn't allocate space for an object. In that sense it doesn't construct the object. When we create an object is the statement

Sample s ;

Compiler emits equivalent Assembly language instructions to allocate space for the object and call the constructor. So constructor is called "after" allocation of space. Thus it doesn't "construct" the object.

This can be proved through the **this** pointer. In our program, the address of object **s** is passed to the constructor and collected in the **this** pointer. We have printed the contents of **this** pointer. You can observe from the sample run that the address contained in the **this** pointer is same as the address of **s** printed in **main( )**.

This means that by the time the control lands in the constructor the object already stands created. The constructor merely initializes an already created object to desired values.

## Challenge 31

Out of constructor and **setData( )** function, which should be preferred to initialize an object?

## Solution

// Project: chall31

```cpp
// Program to illustrate construction versus setData( )
#include <iostream>
using namespace std ;

class Sample
{
    private :
        int i ;
        float a ;

    public :
        Sample ( int j, float b )
        {
            i = j ;
            a = b ;
        }
        void setData ( int x, float y )
        {
            i = x ;
            a = y ;
        }
        void printData( )
        {
            cout << "i = " << i << " a = " << a << endl ;
        }
} ;

int main( )
{
    Sample s ( 10, 3.14 ) ;
    s.printData( ) ;
    s.setData ( 20, 6.28 ) ;
    s.printData( ) ;
    s.setData ( 30, 5.15 ) ;
    s.printData( ) ;

    return 0 ;
}
```

## Sample Run

```
i = 10 a = 3.14
i = 20 a = 6.28
i = 30 a = 5.15
```

## Explanation

In this program both the constructor and **setData( )** are setting values into the object **s**. But the difference is that constructor can be called only once per object. There is no such limit on calls to **setData( )**. So a class often contains both—constructor to initialize the object when it is created and **setData( )** to modify the object as and when required.

## Challenge  32

Can a class contain multiple constructors? If yes, how can they be created and used?

## Solution

```cpp
// Program to illustrate multiple constructors
#include <iostream>
using namespace std ;

class Sample
{
    private :
        int i ;
        float a ;

    public :
        Sample( )
        {
            i = 0 ;
            a = 0.0 ;
        }
```

```
        Sample ( int j, float b )
        {
            i = j ;
            a = b ;
        }
        void printData( )
        {
            cout << "i = " << i << " a = " << a << endl ;
        }
} ;

int main( )
{
    Sample s1, s2 ;
    Sample s3 ( 10, 3.14 ), s4 ( 20, 6.28 ) ;

    s1.printData( ) ;
    s2.printData( ) ;
    s3.printData( ) ;
    s4.printData( ) ;

    return 0 ;
}
```

## Sample Run

```
i = 0 a = 0
i = 0 a = 0
i = 10 a = 3.14
i = 20 a = 6.28
```

## Explanation

Yes, a class can contain multiple constructors. In our **Sample** class we have two—a zero-argument constructor and a two-argument constructor. Such constructors are called overloaded constructors. A suitable constructor is called based on the arguments that we are passing to it. For example, for **s1** and **s2** the zero-argument constructor is called, whereas for **s3** and **s4**, the two-argument constructor is called.

## Challenge  33

Out of multiple constructors in a class which can be dropped and what would be its consequences?

## Solution

```
// Project: chall33
// Program to demonstrate optional constructor
#include <iostream>
using namespace std ;

class Sample
{
    private :
        int i ;
        float a ;

    public :
        Sample( )
        {
            i = 0 ;
            a = 0.0 ;
        }
        Sample ( int j, float b )
        {
            i = j ;
            a = b ;
        }
        void printData( )
        {
            cout << "i = " << i << " a = " << a << endl ;
        }
} ;

int main( )
{
    Sample s1, s2 ;
```

```
        s1.printData( ) ;
        s2.printData( ) ;

        return 0 ;
}
```

## Sample Run

```
i = 0 a = 0
i = 0 a = 0
```

## Explanation

Here we are creating only two objects s1 and s2. They can be constructed using the zero-argument constructor. So even though we are allowed to define the two-argument constructor, since it is not going to be called, we may as well drop it.

Often class in a library contains several constructors to let the user create objects from it in multiple ways.

## Challenge  34

Can a constructor's arguments take default values? If yes, what purpose would it serve?

## Solution

```
// Project: chall34
// Program to illustrate constructor with default values for arguments
#include <iostream>
using namespace std ;

class Sample
{
    private :
        int i ;
        float a ;
```

```
    public :
        Sample ( int j = 0, float b = 0.0 )
        {
            i = j ;
            a = b ;
        }
        void printData( )
        {
            cout << "i = " << i << " a = " << a << endl ;
        }
} ;

int main( )
{
    Sample s1, s2 ;
    Sample s3 ( 10, 3.14 ), s4 ( 20, 6.28 ) ;
    Sample s5 ( 30 ), s6 ( 40 ) ;

    s1.printData( ) ;
    s2.printData( ) ;
    s3.printData( ) ;
    s4.printData( ) ;
    s5.printData( ) ;
    s6.printData( ) ;

    return 0 ;
}
```

## Sample Run

```
i = 0 a = 0
i = 0 a = 0
i = 10 a = 3.14
i = 20 a = 6.28
i = 30 a = 0
i = 40 a = 0
```

## Explanation

A constructor can take default values for its arguments. By using this facility, we could do the job of zero-argument constructor as well as the two-argument constructor in one single constructor.

For **s5** and **s6 i** is set up with values that we passed, whereas **a** is set up with value 0.0.

## Challenge 35

What is the role of a *this* pointer in a constructor?

## Solution

```
// Project: chall35
// Program to illustrate role of this pointer in constructor
#include <iostream>
using namespace std ;

class Sample
{
    private :
        int i ;
        float a ;

    public :
        Sample ( int i = 0, float a = 0.0 )
        {
            cout << "Address of object = " << this << endl ;
            this->i = i ;
            this->a = a ;
        }
        void printData( )
        {
            cout << endl << "Address of object = " << this << endl ;
            cout << "i = " << i << " a = " << a << endl ;
```

```
        }
} ;

int main( )
{
    Sample s1, s2 ;
    Sample s3 ( 10, 3.14 ), s4 ( 20, 6.28 ) ;

    s1.printData( ) ;
    s2.printData( ) ;
    s3.printData( ) ;
    s4.printData( ) ;

    return 0 ;
}
```

## Sample Run

```
Address of object = 0x22cc78
Address of object = 0x22cc70
Address of object = 0x22cc68
Address of object = 0x22cc60

Address of object = 0x22cc78
i = 0 a = 0

Address of object = 0x22cc70
i = 0 a = 0

Address of object = 0x22cc68
i = 10 a = 3.14

Address of object = 0x22cc60
i = 20 a = 6.28
```

## Explanation

A **this** pointer is always passed to the constructor. It contains the address of the object being constructed during that call.

If the names of the arguments and the names of the private variables are same, then using the **this** pointer we can distinguish between private variables and arguments. The ones that are used with **this** pointer are private variable.

## Challenge  36

How to define a Copy constructor?

## Solution

```
// Project: chall36
// Program to demonstrate use of copy constructor
#include <iostream>
using namespace std ;

class Circle
{
    private :
        int radius ;
        float x, y ;

    public :
        Circle( )
        {
        }
        Circle ( int rr, float xx, float yy )
        {
            radius = rr ;
            x = xx ;
            y = yy ;
        }
        Circle ( Circle& c )
        {
            cout << "Copy constructor invoked" << endl ;
            radius = c.radius ;
            x = c.x ;
            y = c.y ;
```

```
        }
        void showData( )
        {
            cout << "Radius = " << radius << endl ;
            cout << "X-Coordinate = " << x << endl ;
            cout << "Y-Coordinate = " << y << endl ;
        }
} ;

int main( )
{
    Circle c1 ( 10, 2.5, 3.5 ) ;
    Circle c2 = c1 ;
    Circle c3 ( c1 ) ;

    c1.showData( ) ;
    c2.showData( ) ;
    c3.showData( ) ;

    return 0 ;
}
```

## Sample Run

```
Copy constructor invoked
Copy constructor invoked
Radius = 10
X-Coordinate = 2.5
Y-Coordinate = 3.5
Radius = 10
X-Coordinate = 2.5
Y-Coordinate = 3.5
Radius = 10
X-Coordinate = 2.5
Y-Coordinate = 3.5
```

## Explanation

Here object **c1** is constructed through the three-argument constructor. Objects **c2** and **c3** are constructed through the copy constructor. **c2** and

**c3** cannot be constructed through the normal three-argument constructor since they are also being initialized where they are defined. Note the different ways of initialization of **c2** and **c3**. Both result into a call to the copy constructor.

Also, note that during both the calls, **c1** is being passed to the copy constructor by reference. Is it necessary for us to use a reference in the argument to the copy constructor? Can we not pass a value instead? No. Because, if we pass the argument by value, its copy is constructed using the copy constructor. This means the copy constructor would call itself to make this copy. This process would go on and on until the compiler runs out of memory. Hence in the copy constructor the argument must always be passed by reference.

Lastly, if we do not provide the copy constructor then the compiler would provide it.

## Challenge 37

What purpose does a copy constructor serve and how is it different than a normal constructor?

## Solution

```
// Project: chall37
// Program to demonstrate cases when copy constructor is called
#include <iostream>
using namespace std ;

class Circle
{
    private :
        int radius ;
        float x, y ;

    public :
        Circle( )
        {
            radius = x = y = 0 ;
        }
```

```
            Circle ( int rr, float xx, float yy )
            {
                radius = rr ;
                x = xx ;
                y = yy ;
            }
            Circle ( const Circle& c )
            {
                cout << "Copy constructor invoked" << endl ;
                radius = c.radius ;
                x = c.x ;
                y = c.y ;
            }
            void showData( )
            {
                cout << "Radius = " << radius << endl ;
                cout << "X-Coordinate = " << x << endl  ;
                cout << "Y-Coordinate = " << y << endl ;
            }
            void setData ( Circle c )
            {
                radius = c.radius ;
                x = c.x ;
                y = c.y ;
            }
    } ;

Circle fun( )
{
    Circle c ;
    return c ;
}

int main( )
{
    Circle c1 ( 10, 2.5, 3.5 ) ;

    Circle c2 = c1 ;
    c2.showData( ) ;

    Circle c3 ;
```

```
        c3.setData ( c1 ) ;
        c3.showData( ) ;

        Circle c4 = fun( ) ;
        c4.showData( ) ;

        return 0 ;
}
```

## Sample Run

```
Copy constructor invoked
Radius = 10
X-Coordinate = 2.5
Y-Coordinate = 3.5
Copy constructor invoked
Radius = 10
X-Coordinate = 2.5
Y-Coordinate = 3.5
Radius = 0
X-Coordinate = 0
Y-Coordinate = 0
```

## Explanation

A copy constructor gets invoked in three situations. These are as follows:

(a) When instantiating one object and initializing it with values from another object.

(b) When passing an object to a function by value.

(c) When an object is returned from a function by value.

When an object is passed by value the copy that the function operates on is created using a copy constructor. If we pass the address or reference of the object, the copy constructor would of course not be invoked, since in these cases the copies of the objects are not to be created.

When an object is returned from a function the copy constructor is invoked to create a copy of the value returned by the function.

However, from the sample run we see that the copy constructor is called only twice—while initializing **c2** and while passing **c1** to **setData( )** function. Contrary to our expectation, it doesn't get called when **c4** is created. This is because the compiler performs a "return value optimization" and eliminates the call to copy constructor to create a copy of the object.

However, in some cases the compiler cannot do this optimization. For example if you change the definition to **fun( )** as shown below and re-execute the program, you would find that this time the copy constructor gets called while returning an object from **fun( )**.

```
Circle fun( )
{
    Circle cthis, cthat ;
    int i = 0 ;

    return ( i ? cthis : cthat ) ;
}
```

# 06 / Total Challenges: 5

# Classes and Objects Challenges

Classes and objects are the heart of and soul of C++ programs. Rarely would you find a worthwhile C++ program that doesn't use classes and objects. Naturally, to be a successful C++ programmer you have to master classes and objects in all their garbs. Challenges in this chapter would test your understanding of them and check whether you can *think* in Object-oriented manner.

## Challenge  38

Write a program to create a class that represents Complex numbers containing real and imaginary parts and then use it to perform complex number addition, subtraction, multiplication and division.

### Solution

```
// Project: chall38
// Program that illustrates various operations on complex numbers
#include <iostream>
#include <cmath>
using namespace std ;

class Complex
{
    private :
        double real ;
        double imag ;

    public :
        Complex( ) ;
        Complex ( double r, double i ) ;
        Complex add ( Complex ) ;
        Complex subtract ( Complex ) ;
        Complex multiply ( Complex ) ;
        Complex divide ( Complex ) ;
        Complex conjugate( ) ;
        double mod( ) ;
        void display( ) ;
} ;

Complex :: Complex( )
{
    real = 0 ;
    imag = 0 ;
}

Complex :: Complex ( double r, double i )
```

```
{
    real = r ;
    imag = i ;
}

Complex Complex :: add ( Complex x )
{
    Complex sum ;

    sum.real = real + x.real ;
    sum.imag = imag + x.imag ;

    return sum ;
}

Complex Complex :: subtract ( Complex x )
{
    Complex res ;

    res.real = real - x.real ;
    res.imag = imag - x.imag ;

    return res ;
}

Complex Complex :: multiply ( Complex x )
{
    Complex prod ;

    prod.real = real * x.real - imag * x.imag ;
    prod.imag = real * x.imag + imag * x.real ;

    return prod ;
}

Complex Complex :: divide ( Complex y )
{
    Complex quo ;

    double mods = y.mod( ) ;
    Complex conj = y.conjugate( ) ;
```

```cpp
        if ( mods == 0 )
            cout << "Unable to divide the complex numbers" << endl ;
        else
        {
            quo = this->multiply ( conj ) ;
            quo.real = quo.real / mods ;
            quo.imag = quo.imag / mods ;
        }

        return quo ;
}

Complex Complex :: conjugate( )
{
    Complex conj ;

    conj.real = real ;
    conj.imag = -imag ;

    return conj ;
}

void Complex :: display( )
{
    cout << "Real part: " << real << endl ;
    cout << "Imaginary part: " << imag << endl ;
    cout << endl ;
}

double Complex :: mod( )
{
    double mod2 = real * real + imag * imag ;
    return sqrt ( mod2 ) ;
}

int main( )
{
    Complex a = Complex ( 2, 3 ) ;
    Complex b ( 6, -1 ) ;
```

```
        cout << "a: " << endl ;
        a.display( ) ;

        cout << "b: " << endl ;
        b.display( ) ;

        cout << "a + b " << endl ;
        Complex c = a.add ( b ) ;
        cout << "Sum: " << endl ;
        c.display( ) ;

        cout << "a - b " << endl ;
        Complex d = a.subtract ( b ) ;
        cout << "Difference: " << endl ;
        d.display( ) ;

        cout << "a * b " << endl ;
        Complex e = a.multiply ( b ) ;
        cout << "Product: " << endl ;
        e.display( ) ;

        cout << "a / b " << endl ;
        Complex f = a.divide ( b ) ;
        cout << "Quotient: " << endl ;
        f.display( ) ;

        return 0 ;
}
```

## Sample Run

```
a:
Real part: 2
Imaginary part: 3

b:
Real part: 6
Imaginary part: -1

a + b
Sum:
```

Real part: 8
Imaginary part: 2

a - b
Difference:
Real part: -4
Imaginary part: 4

a * b
Product:
Real part: 15
Imaginary part: 16

a / b
Quotient:
Real part: 1.47959
Imaginary part: 3.28798

## Explanation

We have firstly declared the **Complex** class containing **real** and **imag** and prototypes of functions required to carry out complex number operations. The definitions of these functions have been done outside the class. Note the use of "::", the scope resolution operator when we define the functions outside the class.

When we make the call

Complex c = a.add ( b ) ;

**b** becomes available in **add( )** function in **x**, whereas, **a** is available through the **this** pointer. So in **add( )** when we use the expression

sum.real = real + x.real ;

**real** represents a's real part.

Same argument applies to other functions as well.

Division of complex numbers is same as multiplying by the conjugate of the divisor, and dividing both the real and imaginary parts by the absolute value of the divisor. The conjugate and absolute values are obtained through the **conjugate( )** and **mod( )** functions respectively. The file **cmath** has been included for the **sqrt( )** function to work.

## Challenge 39

Write a program that performs addition, multiplication, transpose and determinant value operations on 3 x 3 matrices.

## Solution

```cpp
// Project: chall39
// Simulating Matrix Operations
#include <iostream>
#include <cmath>
using namespace std ;

class Matrix
{
    private:
        const static int max = 3 ;
        int arr[ max ][ max ] ;

    public:
        Matrix( ) ;
        void initializeMatrix( ) ;
        void displayMatrix( ) ;
        void add ( Matrix&, Matrix& ) ;
        void multiply ( Matrix&, Matrix& ) ;
        void transpose ( Matrix& ) ;
        int determinant( ) ;
} ;

Matrix :: Matrix( )
{
    for ( int i = 0 ; i < max ; i++ )
    {
        for ( int j = 0 ; j < max ; j++ )
            arr[ i ][ j ] = 0 ;
    }
```

```
}

void Matrix :: initializeMatrix( )
{
    cout << "Enter the contents of the matrix row-wise: " << endl ;

    for ( int i = 0 ; i < max ; i++ )
    {
        cout << "Row " << i << ":" << endl ;
        for ( int j = 0 ; j < max ; j++ )
            cin >> arr[ i ][ j ] ;
        cout << "Row " << i << " completed. " << endl ;
    }

    cout << "Matrix initialized successfully. " << endl ;
}

void Matrix :: displayMatrix( )
{
    for ( int i = 0 ; i < max ; i++ )
    {
        for ( int j = 0 ; j < max ; j++ )
            cout << arr[ i ][ j ] << "\t" ;

        cout << endl ;
    }
}

void Matrix :: add ( Matrix &m1, Matrix &m2 )
{
    for ( int i = 0 ; i < max ; i++ )
    {
        for ( int j = 0 ; j < max ; j++ )
            arr[ i ][ j ] = m1.arr[ i ][ j ] + m2.arr[ i ][ j ] ;
    }
}

void Matrix :: multiply ( Matrix &m1, Matrix &m2 )
{
    for ( int i = 0 ; i < max ; i++ )
    {
```

```
            for ( int j = 0 ; j < max ; j++ )
            {
                int temp ;
                temp = 0 ;
                for ( int k = 0 ; k < max ; k++ )
                    temp = temp + m1.arr[ i ][ k ] * m2.arr[ k ][ j ] ;

                arr[ i ][ j ] = temp ;
            }
        }
}

void Matrix :: transpose ( Matrix &m1 )
{
    for ( int i = 0 ; i < max ; i++ )
    {
        for ( int j = 0 ; j < max ; j++ )
            arr[ i ][ j ] = m1.arr[ j ][ i ] ;
    }
}

int Matrix :: determinant( )
{
    int det ;
    int j, k, p ;

    det = 0 ;
    j = 1 ;
    k = max - 1 ;

    for ( int i = 0 ; i < max ; i++ )
    {
        p = pow ( -1, i ) ;

        if ( i == max - 1 )
            k = 1 ;

        det = det + p * ( arr[ 0 ][ i ] * ( arr[ 1 ][ j ] * arr[ 2 ][ k ] -
                arr[ 2 ][ j ] * arr[ 1 ][ k ] ) ) ;
        j = 0 ;
    }
```

```
        return det ;
}

int main( )
{
    Matrix mat1, mat2, mat3, mat4, mat5 ;

    cout << "Initialize Matrix 1: " << endl ;
    mat1.initializeMatrix( ) ;

    cout << "Initialize Matrix 2: " << endl ;
    mat2.initializeMatrix( ) ;

    cout << "First Matrix: " << endl ;
    mat1.displayMatrix( ) ;

    cout << "Second Matrix: " << endl ;
    mat2.displayMatrix( ) ;

    mat3.add ( mat1, mat2 ) ;
    cout << "After addition: " << endl ;
    mat3.displayMatrix( ) ;

    mat4.multiply ( mat1, mat2 ) ;
    cout << "After multiplication: " << endl ;
    mat4.displayMatrix( ) ;

    mat5.transpose ( mat1 ) ;
    cout << "Transpose of Matrix 1: " << endl ;
    mat5.displayMatrix( ) ;

    cout << "Determinant of Matrix 1: " << mat1.determinant( ) << endl ;

    return 0 ;
}
```

## Sample Run

Initialize Matrix 1:
Enter the contents of the matrix row-wise:

Row 0:
1
2
3
Row 0 completed.
Row 1:
4
5
6
Row 1 completed.
Row 2:
7
8
9
Row 2 completed.
Matrix initialized successfully.
Initialize Matrix 2:
Enter the contents of the matrix row-wise:
Row 0:
1
1
1
Row 0 completed.
Row 1:
1
1
1
Row 1 completed.
Row 2:
1
1
1
Row 2 completed.
Matrix initialized successfully.
First Matrix:
1    2    3
4    5    6
7    8    9
Second Matrix:
1    1    1
1    1    1

```
1    1    1
After addition:
2    3    4
5    6    7
8    9    10
After multiplication:
6    6    6
15   15   15
24   24   24
Transpose of Matrix 1:
1    4    7
2    5    8
3    6    9
Determinant of Matrix 1: 0
```

## Explanation

In this program we have defined some functions that perform different matrix operations like addition, multiplication, transposition, etc. The function **initializeMatrix( )** is used to fill a 2D array of **int**s with values supplied by the user. The **displayMatrix( )** function displays the elements of the matrix.

The function **add( )** adds the elements of two matrices **mat1** and **mat2** and stores the result in the third matrix **mat3.** Similarly, the function **multuiply( )** multiplies the elements of matrix **mat1** with the elements of matrix **mat2** and stores the result in **mat4.**

The function **transpose( )**, transposes a matrix. A transpose of a matrix is obtained by interchanging the rows with corresponding columns of a given matrix. The transposed matrix is stored in **mat5.**

Lastly, we have obtained determinant value of matrix **mat1** through the **determinant( )** function.

## Challenge  40

Write a program to create a class that can calculate the surface area and volume of a solid. The class should also have a provision to accept the data relevant to the solid.

## Solution

```
// Project: chall40
// Program that calculates the surface area and volume of regular solids
#include <iostream>
#include <cmath>
using namespace std ;

enum SolidType
{
    Cube, Cuboid, Cylinder, Cone, Sphere, Hemisphere
} ;

class Solid
{
    private :
        static const double PI ;
        double a ;  // Cube
        double lcu, bcu, hcu ;   // Cuboid
        double rcy, hcy ;  // Right Circular Cylinder
        double rco, hco ;  // Right Circular Cone
        double rsp ;  // Sphere
        double rhsp ;  // Hemisphere
        SolidType s ;
        double v, csa, tsa ;

    public :
        Solid( ) ;
        Solid ( SolidType ) ;
        void surfaceArea( ) ;
        void volume( ) ;
        void display( ) ;
} ;

const double Solid :: PI = 3.14 ;

Solid :: Solid ( SolidType k )
{
    cout << "Solid Type: " ;
    s = k ;
```

```
switch ( s )
{
    case Cube :
        cout << "Cube" << endl ;
        cout << "Enter edge length of cube: " << endl ;
        cin >> a ;

        if ( a <= 0 )
                cout << "Invalid value for edge length" << endl ;

        break ;

    case Cuboid :
        cout << "Cuboid" << endl ;
        cout << "Enter len, breadth and height of cuboid: " << endl ;
        cin >> lcu >> bcu >> hcu ;

        if ( lcu <= 0 || bcu <= 0 || hcu <= 0 )
            cout << "One or more value(s) is/are invalid" << endl ;

        break ;

    case Cylinder :
        cout << "Cylinder" << endl ;
        cout << "Enter radius and height of cylinder: " << endl ;
        cin >> rcy >> hcy ;

        if ( rcy <= 0 || hcy <= 0 )
            cout << "One or more value(s) is/are invalid" << endl ;

        break ;

    case Cone :
        cout << "Cone" << endl ;
        cout << "Enter radius and height of cone: " << endl ;
        cin >> rco >> hco ;

        if ( rco <= 0 || hco <= 0 )
            cout << "One or more value(s) is/are invalid" << endl ;
        break ;
```

```
        case Sphere :
            cout << "Sphere" << endl ;
            cout << "Enter radius of sphere: " << endl ;
            cin >> rsp ;

            if ( rsp <= 0 )
                cout << "Invalid value for radius of sphere" << endl ;

            break ;

        case Hemisphere :
            cout << "Hemisphere" << endl ;
            cout << "Enter radius of hemisphere: " << endl ;
            cin >> rhsp ;

            if ( rhsp <= 0 )
                cout << "Invalid value for radius of hemisphere" << endl ;

            break ;
    }
}

void Solid :: volume( )
{
    switch ( s )
    {
        case Cube :
            v = a * a * a ;
            break ;

        case Cuboid :
            v = lcu * bcu * hcu ;
            break ;

        case Cylinder :
            v = PI * rcy * rcy * hcy ;
            break ;

        case Cone :
            v = ( PI * rco * rco * hco ) / 3.0 ;
```

```
                    break ;

            case Sphere :
                v = ( 4 / 3.0 ) * ( PI * rsp * rsp * rsp ) ;
                break ;

            case Hemisphere :
                v = ( 2 / 3.0 ) * ( PI * rhsp * rhsp * rhsp ) ;
                break ;
        }
}

void Solid :: surfaceArea( )
{
    double lco ;

    switch ( s )
    {
        case Cube :
            csa = 4 * a * a ;
            tsa = 6 * a * a ;
            break ;

        case Cuboid :
            csa = lcu * hcu + bcu * hcu ;
            tsa = lcu * bcu + bcu * hcu + lcu * hcu ;
            break ;

        case Cylinder :
            csa = 2 * PI * rcy * hcy ;
            tsa = csa + 2 * PI * rcy * rcy ;
            break ;

        case Cone :
            lco = sqrt ( rco * rco + hco * hco ) ;
            csa = PI * rco * lco ;
            tsa = csa + PI * rco * rco ;
            break ;

        case Sphere :
            csa = tsa = 4 * PI * rsp * rsp ;
```

```
                break ;

            case Hemisphere :
                csa = 2 * PI * rhsp * rhsp ;
                tsa = 3 * PI * rhsp * rhsp ;
                break ;
        }
}

void Solid :: display( )
{
    switch ( s )
    {
        case Cube :
            cout << "Edge of cube: " << a << endl ;
            break ;

        case Cuboid :
            cout << "Length of cuboid: " << lcu << endl ;
            cout << "Breadth of cuboid: " << bcu << endl ;
            cout << "Height of cuboid: " << hcu << endl ;
            break ;

        case Cylinder :
            cout << "Radius of Cylinder: " << rcy << endl ;
            cout << "Height of Cylinder: " << hcy << endl ;
            break ;

        case Cone :
            cout << "Radius of Cone: " << rco << endl ;
            cout << "Height of Cone: " << hco << endl ;
            break ;

        case Sphere :
            cout << "Radius of Sphere: " << rsp << endl ;
            break ;

        case Hemisphere :
            cout << "Radius of Hemisphere: " << rhsp << endl ;
            break ;
    }
```

```
        cout << "Lateral Surface Area: " << csa << endl ;
        cout << "Total Surface Area: " << tsa << endl ;
        cout << "Volume: " << v << endl ;
}

int main( )
{
        Solid cyl = Solid ( Cylinder ) ;
        cyl.surfaceArea( ) ;
        cyl.volume( ) ;
        cyl.display( ) ;

        Solid cube = Solid ( Cube ) ;
        cube.surfaceArea( ) ;
        cube.volume( ) ;
        cube.display( ) ;

        Solid cub = Solid ( Cuboid ) ;
        cub.surfaceArea( ) ;
        cub.volume( ) ;
        cub.display( ) ;

        Solid con = Solid ( Cone ) ;
        con.surfaceArea( ) ;
        con.volume( ) ;
        con.display( ) ;

        Solid hem = Solid ( Hemisphere ) ;
        hem.surfaceArea( ) ;
        hem.volume( ) ;
        hem.display( ) ;

        Solid sph = Solid ( Sphere ) ;
        sph.surfaceArea( ) ;
        sph.volume( ) ;
        sph.display( ) ;

        return 0 ;
}
```

## Sample Run

Solid Type: Cylinder
Enter radius and height of cylinder:
3
7
Radius of Cylinder: 3
Height of Cylinder: 7
Lateral Surface Area: 131.88
Total Surface Area: 188.4
Volume: 197.82
Solid Type: Cube
Enter edge length of cube:
4
Edge of cube: 4
Lateral Surface Area: 64
Total Surface Area: 96
Volume: 64
Solid Type: Cuboid
Enter length, breadth and height of cuboid:
3
4
5
Length of cuboid: 3
Breadth of cuboid: 4
Height of cuboid: 5
Lateral Surface Area: 35
Total Surface Area: 47
Volume: 60
Solid Type: Cone
Enter radius and height of cone:
6
8
Radius of Cone: 6
Height of Cone: 8
Lateral Surface Area: 188.4
Total Surface Area: 301.44
Volume: 301.44
Solid Type: Hemisphere
Enter radius of hemisphere:

4
Radius of Hemisphere: 4
Lateral Surface Area: 100.48
Total Surface Area: 150.72
Volume: 133.973
Solid Type: Sphere
Enter radius of sphere:
4
Radius of Sphere: 4
Lateral Surface Area: 200.96
Total Surface Area: 200.96
Volume: 267.947

## Explanation

Since we are dealing with multiple types of solids here, to handle the types we have defined an **enum** called **SolidType**. While receiving input (in constructor) or displaying output, or calculating the volume or surface area we have identified the type of solid using the **enum** value stored in **s**.

We have used the standard formulae for calculation of volume, curved surface are (**csa**) and total surface area (**tsa**) of each solid type.

## Challenge 41

Write a program to create a class that can calculate the perimeter / circumference and area of a regular shape. The class should also have a provision to accept the data relevant to the shape.

## Solution

```
// Project: chall41
// Program that calculates the area and circumference of 2D shapes
#include <iostream>
#include <cmath>
using namespace std ;
```

```
enum ShapeType
{
    Square, Rectangle, Triangle, Circle
} ;

class Shape
{
    private :
        double asq ;  // Square
        double lrec, brec ;  // Rectangle
        double atri, btri, ctri ;  // Triangle
        double rci ;  // Circle

        ShapeType s ;
        double peri ;
        double ar ;

        static const double PI ;

    public :
        Shape( ) ;
        Shape ( ShapeType ) ;
        void area( ) ;
        void perimeter( ) ;
        void display( ) ;
} ;

const double Shape :: PI = 22 / 7.0 ;

Shape :: Shape ( ShapeType k )
{
    cout << "Shape Type: " ;
    s = k ;

    switch ( s )
    {
        case Square :
            cout << "Square" << endl ;
            cout << "Enter the side of the square: " << endl ;
            cin >> asq ;
```

```
    if ( asq <= 0 )
        cout << "Invalid value for side of square" << endl ;

    break ;

case Rectangle :
    cout << "Rectangle" << endl ;
    cout << "Enter length & breadth of the rectangle: " << endl ;
    cin >> lrec >> brec ;

    if ( lrec <= 0 || brec <= 0 )
        cout << "One of more value ( s ) is/are invalid" << endl ;

    break ;

case Triangle :
    cout << "Triangle" << endl ;
    cout << "Enter the length of sides of the triangle: " << endl ;
    cin >> atri >> btri >> ctri ;

    if ( atri <= 0 || btri <= 0 || ctri <= 0 )
        cout << "One of more value ( s ) is/are invalid" << endl ;
    else
    {
        double s1 = atri + btri ;
        double s2 = atri + ctri ;
        double s3 = btri + ctri ;

        if ( s1 <= ctri || s2 <= btri || s3 <= atri )
            cout << "The 3 sides do not form a triangle" << endl ;
    }
    break ;

case Circle :
    cout << "Circle" << endl ;
    cout << "Enter the radius of the circle: " << endl ;
    cin >> rci ;

    if ( rci <= 0 )
        cout << "Invalid value for radius of circle" << endl ;
```

```
                break ;
        }
}

void Shape :: perimeter( )
{
    switch ( s )
    {
        case Square :
            peri = 4 * asq ;
            break ;

        case Rectangle :
            peri = 2 * ( lrec + brec ) ;
            break ;

        case Triangle :
            peri = atri + btri + ctri ;
            break ;

        case Circle :
            peri = 2 * PI * rci ;
            break ;
    }
}

void Shape :: area( )
{
    switch ( s )
    {
        case Square :
            ar = asq * asq ;
            break ;

        case Rectangle :
            ar = lrec * brec ;
            break ;

        case Triangle :
        {
            double sp = ( atri + btri + ctri ) / 2.0 ;
```

```
                ar = sqrt ( sp * ( sp - atri ) * ( sp - btri ) * ( sp - ctri ) ) ;
                break ;
        }
        case Circle :
            ar = PI * rci * rci ;
            break ;
    }
}

void Shape :: display( )
{
    switch ( s )
    {
        case Square :
            cout << "Side of square: " << asq << endl ;
            break ;

        case Rectangle :
            cout << "Length of rectangle: " << lrec << endl ;
            cout << "Breadth of rectangle: " << brec << endl ;
            break ;

        case Triangle :
            cout << "Sides of triangle: " << atri << " " << btri << " "
                    << ctri << endl ;
            break ;

        case Circle :
            cout << "Radius of circle: " << rci << endl ;
            break ;
    }

    cout << "Perimeter: " << peri << endl ;
    cout << "Area: " << ar << endl ;
}

int main( )
{
    Shape squ = Shape ( Square ) ;
    squ.perimeter( ) ;
    squ.area( ) ;
```

```
      squ.display( ) ;

      Shape rec = Shape ( Rectangle ) ;
      rec.perimeter( ) ;
      rec.area( ) ;
      rec.display( ) ;

      Shape tri = Shape ( Triangle ) ;
      tri.perimeter( ) ;
      tri.area( ) ;
      tri.display( ) ;

      Shape cir = Shape ( Circle ) ;
      cir.perimeter( ) ;
      cir.area( ) ;
      cir.display( ) ;

      return 0 ;
}
```

## Sample Run

```
Shape Type: Square
Enter the side of the square:
4
Side of square: 4
Perimeter: 16
Area: 16
Shape Type: Rectangle
Enter length & breadth of the rectangle:
6
5
Length of rectangle: 6
Breadth of rectangle: 5
Perimeter: 22
Area: 30
Shape Type: Triangle
Enter the length of sides of the triangle:
6
4
5
```

Sides of triangle: 6 4 5
Perimeter: 15
Area: 9.92157
Shape Type: Circle
Enter the radius of the circle:
3
Radius of circle: 3
Perimeter: 18.8571
Area: 28.2857

## Explanation

Since we are dealing with multiple types of shapes here, to handle the types we have defined an enum called **ShapeType**. While receiving input in the constructor, or displaying output in **display( )**, or in calculating the perimeter in **perimeter( )** or in calculating area in **area( )**, we have identified the type of shape using the enum value stored in **s**.

We have used the standard formulae for calculation of perimeter and area of each shape type.

## Challenge  42

Write a program that creates and uses a time class to perform various time arithmetic.

## Solution

```
// Project: chall42
// Program that performs various time arithmetic
#include <iostream>
using namespace std ;

class Time
{
    private:
        int hour, min, sec ;
```

```
        // If time in AM, amPm is true. If time in PM, amPm is false
        bool amPm ;
        bool format12 ;

    public:
        Time( ) ;
        Time ( int, int, int, bool ) ;
        Time ( int, int, int ) ;
        void displayTime( ) ;
        void convertTo24( ) ;
        void convertTo12( ) ;
} ;

Time :: Time( )
{
    hour = min = sec = 0 ;

    // Default time set to midnight
    // Default time format set to 12 hour
    amPm = true ;
    format12 = true ;
}

// Constructor for 12 hour time format
Time :: Time ( int h, int m, int s, bool aP )
{
    if ( h >= 0 && h <= 12 && m >= 0 && m <= 59 && s >= 0 && s <= 59 )
    {
        hour = h ;
        min = m ;
        sec = s ;
        amPm = aP ;
        format12 = true ;

        if ( hour == 12 && amPm == true )
            hour = 0 ;
    }
    else
    {
        cout << "One or more value(s) are not in valid range" << endl ;
        cout << "Setting time to default" << endl ;
```

```
        hour = 0 ;
        min = 0 ;
        sec = 0 ;
        amPm = true ;
        format12 = true ;
    }
}

// Constructor for 24 hour time format
Time :: Time ( int h, int m, int s )
{
    if ( h >= 0 && h <= 23 && m >= 0 && m <= 59 && s >= 0 && s <= 59 )
    {
        hour = h ;
        min = m ;
        sec = s ;
        format12 = false ;
    }
    else
    {
        cout << "One of more value(s) are not in valid range" << endl ;
        cout << "Setting time to default" << endl ;
        hour = 0 ;
        min = 0 ;
        sec = 0 ;
        amPm = true ;
        format12 = true ;
    }
}

void Time :: convertTo24( )
{
    if ( format12 == true )
    {
        if ( amPm == false )
        {
            if ( hour != 12 )
                hour = hour + 12 ;
        }
    }
    format12 = false ;
```

```
}

void Time :: convertTo12( )
{
    if ( format12 == false )
    {
        if ( hour > 12 )
        {
            hour = hour - 12 ;
            amPm = false ;
        }
        else if ( hour == 12 )
            amPm = false ;
        else
            amPm = true ;
    }
    format12 = true ;
}

void Time :: displayTime( )
{
    cout << "Time: " ;
    if ( format12 == true )
    {
        cout << hour << ":" << min << ":" << sec << " " ;
        if ( amPm == true )
            cout << "AM" << endl ;
        else
            cout << "PM" << endl ;
    }
    else
        cout << hour << ":" << min << ":" << sec << " hrs" << endl ;
}

int main( )
{
    Time t1 ;
    t1.displayTime( ) ;

    Time t2 = Time ( 14, 35, 28 ) ;
    t2.displayTime( ) ;
```

```
        t2.convertTo12( ) ;
        t2.displayTime( ) ;

        Time t3 = Time ( 2, 5, 43, true ) ;
        t3.displayTime( ) ;

        t3.convertTo24( ) ;
        t3.displayTime( ) ;

        return 0 ;
}
```

## Sample Run

Time: 0:0:0 AM
Time: 14:35:28 hrs
Time: 2:35:28 PM
Time: 2:5:43 AM
Time: 2:5:43 hrs

## Explanation

This is a fairly straight-forward program. It has 3 constructors in it. The zero-argument constructor sets the time to midnight and time format to 12 hour format. The other two constructors validate the arguments passed to them and set the time and time format if the arguments are found valid. **convertTo12( )** and **convertTo24( )** converts time from one format to another.

# 07 /

Total Challenges: 6

# More Classes and
# Objects Challenges

**T**his chapter tests your understanding and maturity in developing programs that involve classes and objects.

## Challenge 43

Write a program to create an array class. Make a provision to perform following operations on objects of this class:

Traversal: Processing each element in the array

Search: Finding the location of an element with a given value

Insertion: Adding a new element to an array

Deletion: Removing an element from an array

Sorting: Organizing the elements in some order

Merging: Combining two arrays into a single array

Reversing: Reversing the elements of an array

## Solution

```cpp
// Project: chall43
// Array operations
#include <iostream>
using namespace std ;

const int MAX = 5 ;

class array
{
    private :
        int arr[ MAX ] ;

    public :
        void insert ( int pos, int num ) ;
        void del ( int pos ) ;
        void reverse( ) ;
        void display( ) ;
        void search ( int num ) ;
} ;

// inserts an element num at given position pos
```

```
void array :: insert ( int pos, int num )
{
    int  i ;

    // shift elements to right
    for ( i = MAX - 1 ; i >= pos ; i-- )
        arr[ i ] = arr[ i - 1 ] ;
    arr[ i ] = num ;
}

// deletes an element from the given position pos
void array :: del ( int pos )
{
    int  i ;

    // skip to the desired position
    for ( i = pos ; i < MAX ; i++ )
        arr[ i - 1 ] = arr[ i ] ;
    arr[ i - 1 ] = 0 ;
}

// reverses the entire array
void array :: reverse( )
{
    int  i ;
    for ( i = 0 ; i < MAX / 2 ; i++ )
    {
        int temp = arr[ i ] ;
        arr[ i ] = arr[ MAX - 1 - i ] ;
        arr[ MAX - 1 - i ] = temp ;
    }
}

// searches array for a given element num
void array :: search ( int num )
{
    int  i ;

    // Traverse the array
    for ( i = 0 ; i < MAX ; i++ )
    {
```

```
        if ( arr[ i ] == num )
        {
            cout << "\n\nThe element " << num
                << " is present at " << ( i + 1) << "th position\n" ;
            return ;
        }
    }

    if ( i == MAX )
        cout << "\n\nThe element " << num
            << " is not present in the array\n" ;
}

// displays the contents of an array
void array :: display( )
{
    cout << endl ;
    // traverse the entire array
    for ( int i = 0 ; i < MAX ; i++ )
        cout << "  " << arr[ i ] ;
}

int main( )
{
    array a ;

    a.insert ( 1,11 ) ;
    a.insert ( 2,12 ) ;
    a.insert ( 3,13 ) ;
    a.insert ( 4,14 ) ;
    a.insert ( 5,15 ) ;

    cout << "\nElements of Array: " ;
    a.display( ) ;

    a.del ( 5 ) ;
    a.del ( 2 ) ;
    cout << "\n\nAfter deletion: " ;
    a.display( ) ;

    a.insert ( 2, 222 ) ;
```

```
    a.insert ( 5, 555 ) ;
    cout << "\n\nAfter insertion: " ;
    a.display( ) ;

    a.reverse( ) ;
    cout << "\n\nAfter reversing: " ;
    a.display( ) ;

    a.search ( 222 ) ;
    a.search ( 666 ) ;
    return 0 ;
}
```

## Sample Run

Elements of Array:
11  12  13  14  15

After deletion:
11  13  14  0  0

After insertion:
11  222  13  14  555

After reversing:
555  14  13  222  11

The element 222 is present at 4th position

The element 666 is not present in the array

## Explanation

In this program we have designed a class called **array**. It contains an array **arr** of 5 **int**s. The functions like **insert( )**, **del( )**, **display( )**, **reverse( )** and **search( )** access and manipulate the array **arr**.

The **insert( )** function takes two arguments, the position **pos** at which the new number has to be inserted and the number **num** that has to be inserted. In this function, first through a loop, we have shifted the numbers, from the specified position, one place to the right of their existing position. Then we have placed the number **num** at the vacant place. The insertion of an element has been illustrated in Figure 7.1.

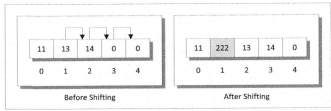

Figure 7.1 Shifting elements while inserting an element at $1^{st}$ position

The **del( )** function deletes the element present at position **pos**. While doing so, we have shifted the numbers placed after the position from where the number is to be deleted one place to the left of their existing positions. The place that is vacant after deletion of an element is filled with 0. The deletion operation has been illustrated in Figure 7.2.

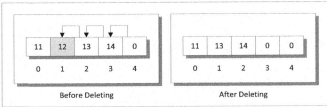

Figure 7.2 Shifting elements to the left while deleting $2^{nd}$ element

In **reverse( )** function, we have reversed the entire array by swapping the elements, like **arr[ 0 ]** with **arr[ 4 ]**, **arr[ 1 ]** with **arr[ 3 ]** and so on. The process of reversing is illustrated in Figure 7.3.

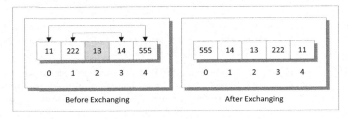

Figure 7.3  Swapping of elements while reversing an array

Note that swapping should continue for **MAX / 2** times only, irrespective of whether **MAX** is even or odd. However, if by mistake the swapping of elements is done for **MAX** times the array would get reversed twice. As a result, the elements would occupy the same place at which they were placed before swapping. In other words, the array would not change.

The **search( )** function searches the array for the specified number. In this function, the 0th element has been compared with the given number **num**. If the element compared happens to be same then the function displays the position at which the number is found. Otherwise, the comparison is carried out until either the list is exhausted or a match is found. If the match is not found then the function displays the relevant message.

In the **display( )** function, the entire array is traversed. As the list is traversed the function displays the elements of the array.

## Challenge 44

Merging of arrays involves two steps—sorting the arrays that are to be merged, and adding the sorted elements of both the arrays to a new array in a sorted order. Write a program that merges two arrays into a third array.

## Solution

```
// Project: chall44
// Merging of arrays
#include <iostream>
using namespace std ;

const int MAX1 = 5 ;
const int MAX2 = 7 ;

class array
{
    private :
```

```
            int *arr ;
            int size ;

        public :

            void create ( int sz ) ;
            void sort( ) ;
            void display( ) ;
            void merge ( array &a , array &b ) ;
    } ;

// creates array of given size sz, dynamically
void array :: create ( int sz )
{
    size = sz ;
    arr = new int[ size ] ;

    int n ;

    for ( int i = 0 ; i < size ; i++ )
    {
        cout << "\nEnter the element no. " << ( i + 1 ) << " " ;
        cin >> n ;
        arr[ i ] = n ;
    }
}

// sorts array in ascending order
void array :: sort( )
{
    int temp ;
    for ( int i = 0 ; i < size ; i++ )
    {
        for ( int j = i + 1 ; j < size ; j++ )
        {
            if ( arr[ i ] > arr[ j ] )
            {
                temp = arr[ i ] ;
                arr[ i ] = arr[ j ] ;
                arr[ j ] = temp ;
            }
```

```
                }
            }
    }

    // displays the contents of array
    void array :: display( )
    {
        for ( int i = 0 ; i < size ; i++)
            cout << " " << arr[ i ] ;
    }

    // merges two arrays of different size
    void array :: merge ( array &a, array &b )
    {
        int i, k, j ;
        size = a.size + b.size ;

        arr = new int[ size ] ;

        for ( k = 0, j = 0, i = 0 ; i <= size ; i++ )
        {
            if ( a.arr[ k ] < b.arr[ j ] )
            {
                arr[ i ] = a.arr[ k ] ;
                k++ ;
                if ( k >= a.size )
                {
                    for ( i++ ; j < b.size ; j++, i++ )
                        arr[ i ] = b.arr[ j ] ;
                }
            }
            else
            {
                arr[ i ] = b.arr[ j ] ;
                j++ ;
                if ( j >= b.size )
                {
                    for ( i++ ; k < a.size ; k++, i++ )
                        arr[ i ] = a.arr[ k ] ;
                }
            }
```

```
    }
}

int main( )
{
    array a ;
    cout << "\nEnter elements for first array: \n" ;
    a.create ( MAX1 ) ;

    array b ;
    cout << "\nEnter elements for second array: \n" ;
    b.create ( MAX2 ) ;

    a.sort( ) ;
    b.sort( ) ;

    cout << "\nFirst array: \n" ;
    a.display( ) ;
    cout << "\n\nSecond array: \n" ;
    b.display( ) ;
    cout << "\n\nAfter Merging: \n" ;

    array c ;
    c.merge ( a, b ) ;
    c.display( ) ;

    return 0 ;
}
```

## Sample Run

Enter elements for first array:

Enter the element no. 1 67
Enter the element no. 2 12
Enter the element no. 3 -4
Enter the element no. 4 43
Enter the element no. 5 2

Enter elements for second array:

Enter the element no. 1 8
Enter the element no. 2 10
Enter the element no. 3 -2
Enter the element no. 4 39
Enter the element no. 5 6
Enter the element no. 6 7
Enter the element no. 7 19

First array:
-4  2  12  43  67

Second array:
-2  6  7  8  10  19  39

After Merging:
-4  -2  2  6  7  8  10  12  19  39  43  67

## Explanation

In this program we have designed a class called **array**. This class contains functions like **create( )** to create an array of **int**s, **sort( )** to sort the elements of an array in ascending order, **merge( )** to add elements of two arrays to the new array and **display( )** to display the contents of an array.

In the class **array**, we have not declared the array **arr** as **arr[ MAX ]** as done in the Challenge 43. This is because the size of the array is different for each object of the class **array** that we wish to use in the program. When the size of the array is not known while declaring it, we declare it as a pointer. To create the array of desired size we have passed either **MAX1** or **MAX2** to the **create( )** function. The array is then created dynamically using operator **new**.

In **merge( )** function, a **for** loop runs for **size** number of times. Here **size** is the sum of the number of elements present in the arrays of objects **a** and **b** respectively. Before placing the element in the new array **arr** we have sequentially compared the elements of two arrays **a.arr** and **b.arr** respectively. The element that is found to be smaller is added first to the array **arr**. Thus, for example, if **a.arr[ k ]** is smaller than **b.arr[ j ]** then **a.arr[ k ]** would get copied to **arr[ i ]** and **k** would get incremented by 1. The element **b.arr[ j ]** would then get compared with the new element

**a.arr[ k ]**. While comparing if any of the two arrays get exhausted, then the remaining elements of the other array would get copied to the array **arr**.

On execution, the program would ask to enter 5 integers for the array belonging to object **a** and 7 integers for the array belonging to object **b**.

## Challenge 45

Design a class called **Rectangle** containing data members top, left, bottom, right to represent its coordinates. Implement the following functions in the **Rectangle** class.

areaPeri( )        Returns area and perimeter of Rectangle

topLeft( )         Returns the top-left point of Rectangle

bottomRight( )  Returns the bottom-right point of Rectangle

centerPoint( )   Returns the center point of the Rectangle

deflateRect( )   Decreases the width and height of the Rectangle

inflateRect( )    Increases the width and height of the Rectangle

equalRect( )      Determines whether a Rectangle is equal to another

height( )          Calculates the height of the Rectangle

width( )           Calculates the width of Rectangle

isRectEmpty( )  Checks if Rectangle is empty (width and/or height = 0)

isRectNull( )     Determines whether all data member are all equal to 0

ptInRect( )       Checks if a specified point lies within the Rectangle

setRect( )        Sets the dimensions of the Rectangle

setRectEmpty   Sets Rectangle to an empty rectangle (all coordinates 0)

size( )            Calculates the size of the Rectangle

intersectRect()  Sets Rectangle equal to intersection of two Rectangles

unionRect( )     Sets Rectangle equal to union of two Rectangles

## Solution

```
// Project: chall45
// Rectangle and its operations
#include <iostream>
using namespace std ;

float max ( float, float ) ;
float min ( float, float ) ;

class Point
{
    private :
        float x, y ;

    public :

        Point ( float xcoordinate, float ycoordinate )
        {
            x = xcoordinate ;
            y = ycoordinate ;
        }

        void displayCoordinates( )
        {
            cout << x << "," << y << endl ;
        }

        float getx( )
        {
            return x ;
        }

        float gety( )
        {
            return y ;
        }
} ;

class Rectangle
```

```
{
    private :

        float top, bottom, left, right ;

    public :

        void areaPeri ( float *aa, float *pp )
        {
            float area, perimeter ;

            *aa = ( bottom - top ) * ( right - left ) ;
            *pp = 2 * ( ( bottom - top ) + ( right - left ) ) ;
        }

        Point topLeft( )
        {
            Point topleftpt ( left, top ) ;
            return topleftpt ;
        }

        Point bottomRight( )
        {
            Point bottomrtpt ( right, bottom ) ;
            return bottomrtpt ;
        }

        Point centerPoint( )
        {
            float x, y, height, width ;

            height = bottom - top ;
            width = right - left ;
            x = top + height/2 ;
            y = left + width/2 ;
            Point center ( x, y ) ;

            return center ;
        }

        void deflateRect ( float y, float x )
```

```
    {
        // Decrease size of rectangle equally from all sides
        // After deflateRect( ), center remains same
        top = top + y/2 ;
        bottom = bottom - y/2 ;
        left = left + x/2 ;
        right = right - x/2 ;
    }

    void inflateRect ( float y, float x )
    {
        // Increase size of rectangle equally from all sides
        // After inflateRect( ), center remains same
        top = top - y/2 ;
        bottom = bottom + y/2 ;
        left = left - x/2 ;
        right = right + x/2 ;
    }

    bool equalRect ( Rectangle otherRect )
    {
        float height1, height2, width1, width2 ;

        height1 = bottom - top ;
        height2 = otherRect.bottom - otherRect.top ;
        width1 = right - left ;
        width2 = otherRect.right - otherRect.left ;
        if ( ( ( height1 == height2 ) && ( width1 == width2 ) ) ||
            ( ( height1 == width2 ) && ( width1 == height2 ) ) )
            return true ;
        else
            return false ;
    }

    float height( )
    {
        return ( bottom - top ) ;
    }

    float width( )
    {
```

```
        return ( right - left ) ;
}

bool isRectEmpty( )
{
    float height, width ;

    height = top - bottom ;
    width = right - left ;

    if ( ( height == 0 ) || ( width == 0 ) )
        return true ;
    else
        return false ;
}

bool isRectNull( )
{
    if ( ( top == 0 ) && ( bottom == 0 ) &&
        ( right == 0 ) && ( left == 0 ) )
        return true ;
    else
        return false ;
}

bool ptInRect ( Point pt )
{
    float xcoord = pt.getx( ) ;
    float ycoord = pt.gety( ) ;

    if ( ( ycoord > top ) && ( ycoord < bottom ) &&
        ( xcoord > left ) && ( xcoord < right ) )
        return true ;
    else
        return false ;
}

void setRect ( float y1, float y2, float x1, float x2 )
{
    if ( ( y1 <= y2 ) && ( x1 <= x2 ) )
    {
```

```
            top = y1 ;
            bottom = y2 ;
            left = x1 ;
            right = x2 ;
        }
        else
            cout << "Invalid coordinates" << endl ;
    }

    void setRectEmpty( )
    {
        top = bottom = left = right = 0 ;
    }

    void intersectRect ( Rectangle rect1, Rectangle rect2 )
    {
        //Check whether the given two rectangles are intersecting
        if ( ( rect1.right > rect2.left ) && ( rect1.left < rect2.right ) &&
            ( rect1.top < rect2.bottom ) && ( rect1.bottom > rect2.top ))
        {
            top = max ( rect1.top, rect2.top ) ;
            bottom = min ( rect1.bottom, rect2.bottom ) ;
            left = max ( rect1.left, rect2.left ) ;
            right = min ( rect1.right, rect2.right ) ;
        }
        else
            cout << "Non-intersection rectangles entered" << endl ;
    }

    void unionRect ( Rectangle rect1, Rectangle rect2 )
    {
        if ( ( rect1.top == rect2.top ) &&
            ( rect1.bottom == rect2.bottom ) )
        {
            top = rect1.top ;
            bottom = rect1.bottom ;
            left = min ( rect1.left, rect2.left ) ;
            right = max ( rect1.right, rect2.right ) ;
        }
        else
            cout << "Union is not a rectangle" << endl ;
```

```
        }
} ;

float min ( float n1, float n2 )
{
    return ( n1 <= n2 ? n1 : n2 ) ;
}

float max ( float n1, float n2 )
{
    return ( n1 >= n2 ? n1 : n2 ) ;
}

int main( )
{
    Rectangle r1, r2, r3, r4 ;
    float area, perimeter ;

    r1.setRect ( 1, 3, 1, 3 ) ;
    r2.setRect ( 1, 3, 1.5, 3.5 ) ;

    r1.areaPeri ( &area, &perimeter ) ;
    cout << "Area = " << area << endl ;
    cout << "Perimeter = " << perimeter << endl ;

    Point topleftpoint = r1.topLeft( ) ;
    Point bottomrightpoint = r1.bottomRight( ) ;
    Point center = r1.centerPoint( ) ;
    cout << "Top Left : " << endl ;
    topleftpoint.displayCoordinates( ) ;
    cout << "Bottom Right : " << endl ;
    bottomrightpoint.displayCoordinates( ) ;
    cout << "Center : " << endl ;
    center.displayCoordinates( ) ;

    bool equal = r1.equalRect ( r2 ) ;
    cout << "Equality : " << equal << endl ;

    float h = r1.height( ) ;
    float w = r1.width( ) ;
    cout << "Height : " << h << endl ;
```

```
cout << "Width : " << w << endl ;

bool empty = r1.isRectEmpty( ) ;
cout << "Empty : " << empty << endl ;

bool null = r1.isRectNull( ) ;
cout << "Null : " << null << endl ;

Point point1 ( 2, 1.5 ), point2 ( 0.5, 0.5 ) ;
bool point1bool = r1.ptInRect ( point1 ) ;
bool point2bool = r1.ptInRect ( point2 ) ;
cout << "Point 1 in Rectangle : " << point1bool << endl ;
cout << "Point 2 in Rectangle : " << point2bool << endl ;

r3.intersectRect ( r1, r2 ) ;
Point r3topleft = r3.topLeft( ) ;
cout << "Top Left of Intersection : " << endl ;
r3topleft.displayCoordinates( ) ;
Point r3bottomright = r3.bottomRight( ) ;
cout << "Bottom Right of Intersection : " << endl ;
r3bottomright.displayCoordinates( ) ;

r4.unionRect ( r1, r2 ) ;
Point r4topleft = r4.topLeft( ) ;
cout << "Top Left of Union : " << endl ;
r4topleft.displayCoordinates( ) ;
Point r4bottomright = r4.bottomRight( ) ;
cout << "Bottom Right of Union : " << endl ;
r4bottomright.displayCoordinates( ) ;

r1.inflateRect ( 1,1 ) ;
topleftpoint = r1.topLeft( ) ;
bottomrightpoint = r1.bottomRight( ) ;
center = r1.centerPoint( ) ;
cout << "Top Left : " << endl ;
topleftpoint.displayCoordinates( ) ;
cout << "Bottom Right : " << endl ;
bottomrightpoint.displayCoordinates( ) ;
cout << "Center : " << endl ;
center.displayCoordinates( ) ;
```

```
    r1.deflateRect ( 1,1 ) ;
    topleftpoint = r1.topLeft( ) ;
    bottomrightpoint = r1.bottomRight( ) ;
    center = r1.centerPoint( ) ;
    cout << "Top Left : " << endl ;
    topleftpoint.displayCoordinates( ) ;
    cout << "Bottom Right : " << endl ;
    bottomrightpoint.displayCoordinates( ) ;
    cout << "Center : " << endl ;
    center.displayCoordinates( ) ;

    return 0 ;
}
```

## Sample Run

```
Area = 4
Perimeter = 8
Top Left :
1,1
Bottom Right :
3,3
Center :
2,2
Equality : 1
Height : 2
Width : 2
Empty : 0
Null : 0
Point 1 in Rectangle : 1
Point 2 in Rectangle : 0
Top Left of Intersection :
1.5,1
Bottom Right of Intersection :
3,3
Top Left of Union :
1,1
Bottom Right of Union :
3.5,3
Top Left :
0.5,0.5
```

Bottom Right :
3.5,3.5
Center :
2,2
Top Left :
1,1
Bottom Right :
3,3
Center :
2,2

## Explanation

The program is pretty self-explanatory, as the functions of **Rectangle** class are simple. Apart from the **Ractangle** class we have also defined the **Point** class to get, set and display coordinates of a point.

## Challenge 46

Write a program to check whether a 3 x 3 matrix is a singular matrix or an orthogonal matrix, etc.

## Solution

```
// Project: chall46
// Singular / Orthogonal matrix
#include <iostream.h>
#include <math.h>
using namespace std ;

const int MAX = 3 ;

class matrix
{
    private :

        int mat[ MAX ][ MAX ] ;
```

```
    public :

        matrix( ) ;
        void create( ) ;
        void display( ) ;
        matrix matmul ( matrix &m ) ;
        matrix transpose( ) ;
        int determinant( ) ;
        int isortho( ) ;
} ;

// initializes the matrix mat with 0
matrix :: matrix( )
{
    for ( int i = 0 ; i < MAX ; i++ )
    {
        for ( int j = 0 ; j < MAX ; j++ )
            mat[ i ][ j ] = 0 ;
    }
}

// creates matrix mat
void matrix :: create( )
{
    int n ;
    for ( int i = 0 ; i < MAX ; i++ )
    {
        for ( int j = 0 ; j < MAX ; j++ )
        {
            cout << "\nEnter the element: " ;
            cin >> n ;
            mat[ i ][ j ] = n ;
        }
    }
}

// displays the contents of matrix
void matrix :: display( )
{
    for ( int i = 0 ; i < MAX ; i++ )
    {
```

```cpp
            for ( int j = 0 ; j < MAX ; j++ )
                cout << mat[ i ][ j ] << " " ;
            cout << endl ;
    }
}

// multiplies two matrices
matrix matrix :: matmul ( matrix &m )
{
    matrix m1 ;
    for ( int k = 0 ; k < MAX ; k++ )
    {
        for ( int i = 0 ; i < MAX ; i++ )
        {
            for ( int j = 0 ; j < MAX ; j++ )
                m1.mat[ k ][ i ] += mat[ k ][ j ] * m.mat[ j ][ i ] ;
        }
    }
    return m1 ;
}

// obtains transpose of matrix
matrix matrix :: transpose( )
{
    matrix m ;
    for ( int i = 0 ; i < MAX ; i++ )
    {
        for ( int j = 0 ; j < MAX ; j++ )
        m.mat[ i ][ j ] = mat[ j ][ i ] ;
    }
    return m ;
}

// finds the determinant value for given matrix
int matrix :: determinant( )
{
    int sum, j, k, p ;
    sum = 0 ; j = 1 ; k = MAX - 1 ;

    for ( int i = 0 ; i < MAX ; i++ )
    {
```

```
        p = pow ( -1, i ) ;

        if ( i == MAX - 1 )
            k = 1 ;
        sum = sum + ( mat[ 0 ][ i ] * ( mat[ 1 ][ j ] *
                    mat[ 2 ][ k ] - mat[ 2 ][ j ] *
                    mat[ 1 ][ k ] ) ) * p ;
        j = 0 ;
    }

    return sum ;
}

// checks if given matrix is an orthogonal matrix
int matrix :: isortho( )
{
    // transpose the matrix ;
    matrix m1 = transpose( ) ;

    // multiply the matrix with its transpose
    matrix m2 = matmul ( m1 ) ;

    // check for the identity matrix
    for ( int i = 0 ; i < MAX ; i++ )
    {
        if ( m2.mat[ i ][ i ] == 1 )
            continue ;
        else
            break ;
    }
    if ( i == MAX )
        return 1 ;
    else
        return 0 ;
}

void main( )
{
    matrix mat1 ;
    cout << "\nEnter elements for first array: \n" ;
    mat1.create( ) ;
```

```
    cout << "\nThe Matrix: " << endl ;
    mat1.display( ) ;

    int d = mat1.determinant( ) ;
    cout << "\nThe determinant for given matrix: " << d << endl ;

    if ( d == 0 )
        cout << "\nmat1 matrix is singular" << endl ;
    else
        cout << "\nmat1 matrix is not singular" << endl ;

    d = mat1.isortho( ) ;
    if ( d != 0 )
        cout << "\nmat1 matrix is orthogonal" << endl ;
    else
        cout << "\nmat1 matrix is not orthogonal" << endl ;
}
```

## Sample Run

Enter elements for first array:

Enter the element: 1
Enter the element: 0
Enter the element: 0
Enter the element: 0
Enter the element: 1
Enter the element: 0
Enter the element: 0
Enter the element: 0
Enter the element: 1

The Matrix:
1 0 0
0 1 0
0 0 1

The determinant for given matrix: 1
mat1 matrix is not singular
mat1 matrix is orthogonal

## Explanation

In this program, in addition to functions **create( )**, **display( )**, **matmul( )**, and **transpose( )**, the class **matrix** contains functions like **determinant( )** and **isortho( )**.

The **determinant( )** function calculates the determinant value for a given matrix. Here, the matrix for which the determinant value has to be calculated is a square matrix. A square matrix is the one in which the number of rows is equal to the number of columns. We have calculated the determinant value through a loop as shown below:

In $1^{st}$ iteration when i = 0:

```
p = pow ( -1, 0 ) ;
sum = sum + ( mat[ 0 ][ 0 ] * ( mat[ 1 ][ 1 ] * mat[ 2 ][ 2 ] −
            mat[ 2 ][ 1 ] * mat[ 1 ][ 2 ] ) ) * p ;
    = 0 + ( 1 * ( 1 * 1 - 0 * 0 ) ) * 1 ;
    = 1
```

In $2^{nd}$ iteration when i = 1:

```
p = pow ( -1, 1 ) ;
sum = sum + ( mat[ 0 ][ 1 ] * ( mat[ 1 ][ 0 ] * mat[ 2 ][ 2 ] −
            mat[ 2 ][ 0 ] * mat[ 1 ][ 2 ] ) ) * p ;
    = 1 + ( 0 * ( 0 * 1 - 0 * 0 ) ) * -1 ;
    = 1
```

In 3rd iteration when i = 2:

```
p = pow ( -1, 2 ) ;
sum = sum + ( mat[ 0 ][ 2 ] * ( mat[ 1 ][ 0 ] * mat[ 2 ][ 1 ] −
            mat[ [ 2 ][ 0 ] * mat[ 1 ][ 1 ] ) ) * p ;
    = 1 + ( 0 * ( 0 * 0 - 0 * 1 ) ) * 1 ;
    = 1
```

A matrix is called **singular** if the determinant value of a matrix is 0. The determinant value for the matrix that we have keyed in is 1 hence it is not a singular matrix.

The **isortho( )** function checks whether or not a given matrix is orthogonal. A square matrix is said to be **orthogonal**, if the matrix obtained by multiplying the matrix with its transpose is an identity matrix. In other words, if A is a matrix and T is its transpose, then matrix B obtained by multiplying A with T is called orthogonal if it is an identity matrix. An identity matrix is a square matrix in which the elements in the leading diagonal are 1.

Hence in the **isortho( )** function, first we have called the **transpose( )** function to obtain the transpose of the given matrix, and the resultant matrix has been stored in **m1**. Then we have called the **matmul( )** function to obtain the product of the matrix and its transpose. The resultant matrix has been collected in **m2**. Then, through a loop we have checked if the matrix **m2** is an identity matrix or not and returned a suitable value.

## Challenge 47

An expression like $5X^4 + 2X^3 + 7X^2 + 10X - 8$ is called a Polynomial. Write a program to implement addition of two such polynomials.

## Solution

```
// Project: chall47
// Addition of polynomials
#include <iostream>
using namespace std ;

const int MAX = 10 ;

class poly
{
    private :

        struct term
        {
            int coeff ;
            int exp ;
        } t[ MAX ] ;
        int noofterms ;

    public :

        poly( ) ;
```

```
        void polyappend ( int c, int e ) ;
        void polyadd ( poly &p1, poly &p2 ) ;
        void display( ) ;
} ;

// initializes data members of class poly
poly :: poly( )
{
    noofterms = 0 ;
    for ( int i = 0 ; i < MAX ; i++ )
    {
        t[ i ].coeff = 0 ;
        t[ i ].exp = 0 ;
    }
}

// adds the term of polynomial to the array t
void poly :: polyappend ( int c, int e )
{
    t[ noofterms ].coeff = c ;
    t[ noofterms ].exp =  e ;
    noofterms++ ;
}

// displays the polynomial equation
void poly :: display( )
{
    int flag = 0 ;
    for ( int i = 0 ; i < noofterms ; i++ )
    {
        if ( t[ i ].exp != 0 )
            cout << t[ i ].coeff << "x^" << t[ i ].exp  << " + " ;
        else
        {
            cout << t[ i ].coeff ;
            flag = 1 ;
        }
    }
    if ( !flag )
        cout << "\b\b  " ;
}
```

```
// adds two polynomials p1 and p2
void poly :: polyadd ( poly& p1, poly& p2 )
{
    int c = p1.noofterms > p2.noofterms ? p1.noofterms : p2.noofterms ;

    for ( int i = 0, j = 0 ; i <= c ; noofterms++ )
    {
        if ( p1.t[ i ].coeff == 0 && p2.t[ j ].coeff == 0 )
            break ;
        if ( p1.t[ i ].exp >= p2.t[ j ].exp )
        {
            if ( p1.t[ i ].exp == p2.t[ j ].exp )
            {
                t[ noofterms ].coeff = p1.t[ i ].coeff + p2.t[ j ].coeff ;
                t[ noofterms ].exp = p1.t[ i ].exp ;
                i++ ;
                j++ ;
            }
            else
            {
                t[ noofterms ].coeff = p1.t[ i ].coeff ;
                t[ noofterms ].exp = p1.t[ i ].exp ;
                i++ ;
            }
        }
        else
        {
            t[ noofterms ].coeff = p2.t[ j ].coeff ;
            t[ noofterms ].exp = p2.t[ j ].exp ;
            j++ ;
        }
    }
}

int main( )
{
    poly p1 ;

    p1.polyappend ( 1, 7 ) ;
    p1.polyappend ( 2, 6 ) ;
```

```
p1.polyappend ( 3, 5 ) ;
p1.polyappend ( 4, 4 ) ;
p1.polyappend ( 5, 2 ) ;

poly p2 ;
p2.polyappend ( 1, 4 ) ;
p2.polyappend ( 1, 3 ) ;
p2.polyappend ( 1, 2 ) ;
p2.polyappend ( 1, 1 ) ;
p2.polyappend ( 2, 0 ) ;

poly p3 ;
p3.polyadd ( p1, p2 ) ;

cout << endl << "First polynomial:" << endl ;
p1.display( ) ;

cout << endl << "Second polynomial:" << endl ;
p2.display( ) ;

cout << endl << "Resultant polynomial:" << endl ;
p3.display( ) ;

return 0 ;
}
```

## Sample Run

```
First polynomial:
1x^7 + 2x^6 + 3x^5 + 4x^4 + 5x^2
Second polynomial:
1x^4 + 1x^3 + 1x^2 + 1x^1 + 2
Resultant polynomial:
1x^7 + 2x^6 + 3x^5 + 5x^4 + 1x^3 + 6x^2 + 1x^1 + 2
```

## Explanation

In this program, the class **poly** contains a structure called **term**. This structure stores the coefficient and exponent of the term of a polynomial. The data member **nooterms** stores the total number of terms that an object of **poly** class is supposed to hold. The function **polyappend( )** adds the term of a polynomial to the array **t**. It is assumed that the exponent of each successive term is less than that of the previous term.

The function **polyadd( )** adds the polynomials represented by the two objects **p1** and **p2**. The function **display( )** displays the polynomial.

In **main( )**, we have called the function **polyappend( )** several times to build the two polynomials which are represented by the objects **p1** and **p2**. Next, the function **polyadd( )** is called through the object **p3** to carry out the addition of two polynomials. In this function, arrays representing the two polynomials are traversed. While traversing, the polynomials are compared on a term-by-term basis. If the exponents of the two terms being compared are equal then their coefficients are added and the result is stored in the third polynomial. If the exponents of two terms are not equal then the term with the bigger exponent is added to the third polynomial. If the term with an exponent is present in one of the objects of **poly**, then that term is added as it is to the third polynomial.

Lastly, the terms of the resulting polynomial are displayed using the function **display( )**.

## Challenge 48

Write a program that carries out multiplication of two polynomials.

## Solution

```
// Project: chall48
// Polynomial multiplication
#include <stdio.h>
#include <iostream>
using namespace std ;

const int MAX = 10 ;

class poly
{
```

```
private :

    struct term
    {
        int coeff ;
        int exp ;
    } t[ MAX ] ;
    int noofterms ;

public :

    poly( ) ;
    void polyappend ( int c, int e ) ;
    void polyadd ( poly &p1, poly &p2 ) ;
    void polymul ( poly &p1, poly &p2 ) ;
    void display( ) ;
} ;

// initializes data members of class poly
poly :: poly( )
{
    noofterms = 0 ;
    for ( int i = 0 ; i < MAX ; i++ )
    {
        t[ i ].coeff = 0 ;
        t[ i ].exp = 0 ;
    }
}

// adds the term of polynomial to the array t
void poly :: polyappend ( int c, int e )
{
    t[ noofterms ].coeff = c ;
    t[ noofterms ].exp = e ;
    noofterms++ ;
}

// displays the polynomial equation
void poly :: display( )
{
    int flag = 0 ;
```

```
        for ( int i = 0 ; i < noofterms ; i++ )
        {
            if ( t[ i ].exp != 0 )
                cout << t[ i ].coeff << "x^" << t[ i ].exp  << " + " ;
            else
            {
                cout << t[ i ].coeff ;
                flag = 1 ;
            }
        }
        if ( !flag )
            cout << "\b\b  " ;
}

// add two polynomials p1 and p2
void poly :: polyadd ( poly &p1, poly &p2 )
{
    int coeff, exp ;
    poly p ;

    int c = p1.noofterms ;
    int d = p2.noofterms ;

    for ( int i = 0, j = 0 ; i <= c || j <= d ; )
    {
        if ( p1.t[ i ].coeff == 0 && p2.t[ j ].coeff == 0 )
            break ;
        if ( p1.t[ i ].exp >= p2.t[ j ].exp )
        {
            if ( p1.t[ i ].exp == p2.t[ j ].exp )
            {
                coeff = p1.t[ i ].coeff + p2.t[ j ].coeff ;
                exp = p1.t[ i ].exp ;
                i++ ;
                j++ ;
            }
            else
            {
                coeff = p1.t[ i ].coeff ;
                exp = p1.t[ i ].exp ;
                i++ ;
```

```
            }
        }
        else
        {
            coeff = p2.t[ j ].coeff ;
            exp = p2.t[ j ].exp ;
            j++ ;
        }
        p.polyappend ( coeff, exp ) ;
    }
    *this = p ;
}

// multiply two polynomials p1 and p2
void poly :: polymul ( poly &p1, poly &p2 )
{
    int coeff, exp ;
    poly t1, t2 ;

    if ( p1.noofterms != 0 && p2.noofterms != 0 )
    {
        for ( int i = 0 ; i < p1.noofterms ; i++ )
        {
            poly p ;
            for ( int j = 0 ; j < p2.noofterms ; j++ )
            {
                coeff = p1.t[ i ].coeff * p2.t[ j ].coeff ;
                exp = p1.t[ i ].exp + p2.t[ j ].exp ;
                p.polyappend ( coeff, exp ) ;
            }

            if ( i != 0 )
            {
                t2.polyadd ( t1, p ) ;
                t1 = t2 ;
            }
            else
                t1 = p ;
        }

        *this = t2 ;
```

```
        }
    }

    int main( )
    {
        poly p1 ;

        p1.polyappend ( 1, 4 ) ;
        p1.polyappend ( 2, 3 ) ;
        p1.polyappend ( 2, 2 ) ;
        p1.polyappend ( 2, 1 ) ;

        poly p2 ;
        p2.polyappend ( 2, 3 ) ;
        p2.polyappend ( 3, 2 ) ;
        p2.polyappend ( 4, 1 ) ;

        poly p3 ;
        p3.polymul( p1, p2 ) ;

        cout << endl << "First polynomial: " << endl  ;
        p1.display( ) ;

        cout << endl << "Second polynomial: " << endl ;
        p2.display( ) ;

        cout << endl << "Resultant polynomial: " << endl ;
        p3.display( ) ;

        return 0 ;
    }
```

## Sample Run

First polynomial:
1x^4 + 2x^3 + 2x^2 + 2x^1
Second polynomial:
2x^3 + 3x^2 + 4x^1
Resultant polynomial:
2x^7 + 7x^6 + 14x^5 + 18x^4 + 14x^3 + 8x^2

## Explanation

To carry out multiplication of two given polynomial equations, the **poly** class contains one more function **polymul( )**.

As done in Challenge 47, here too we have called the **polyappend( )** function several times to build the two polynomials which are represented by the objects **p1** and **p2**. Next, the function **polymul( )** is called through the object **p3** to carry out the multiplication of two polynomials.

In the **polymul( )** function, first we have checked if the two objects **p1** and **p2** are non-empty. If they are not, then the control enters a pair of **for** loops. Here each term of first polynomial contained in **p1** is multiplied with every term of second polynomial contained in **p2**. While doing so we have called **polyappend( )** to add the terms to **p**. The first resultant polynomial is stored in temporary object **t1** of **poly** class. There onwards the function **polyadd( )** is called to add the resulting polynomial polynomials.

Lastly, the terms of the resulting polynomial are displayed using the function **display( )**.

# 08 / Total Challenges: 6

# Function Challenges

**F**unctions in C++ are more mature as compared to C. C++ has added several new features to them. The challenges in this chapter would test whether you have understood all these new nuances about functions.

YASHAVANT & ADITYA KANETKAR'S

**101 Challenges**

**In C++ Programming**

Solve 101 Challenges to hone C++ Programming skills
Practise them to be a mature C++ programmer

## Challenge  49

Write a program that contains a class **Sample** with three function in it **fun1( )**, **fun2( )** and **fun3( )**. All 3 functions receive an **int** and a **float**. **fun1( )** receives them by value, **fun2( )** by address and **fun3( )** by reference. All of them increment the **int** and **float** by 1. Which function would be able to change the original value of **int** and **float**? Can these functions be defined as overloaded functions?

## Solution

```
// Project: chall49
// Different types of function calls in C++
#include <iostream>
using namespace std ;

class Sample
{
    public :
        void fun1 ( int x, float y )
        {
            x++ ;
            y++;
        }

        void fun2 ( int *x, float *y )
        {
            (*x)++ ;
            (*y)++ ;
        }

        void fun3 ( int &x, float &y )
        {
            x++ ;
            y++;
        }
} ;

int main( )
```

```
{
    int i = 10 ;
    float f = 20 ;

    Sample s ;

    s.fun1 ( i, f ) ;
    cout << "Integer: " << i << " Float: " << f << endl ;

    s.fun2 ( &i, &f ) ;
    cout << "Integer: " << i << " Float: " << f << endl ;

    s.fun3 ( i, f ) ;
    cout << "Integer: " << i << " Float: " << f << endl ;

    return 0 ;
}
```

## Sample Run

```
Integer: 10 Float: 20
Integer: 11 Float: 21
Integer: 12 Float: 22
```

## Explanation

As you can see, **fun1( )** is called by value, **fun2( )** by address and **fun3( )** by reference. Of these, the changes made in **fun2( )** and **fun3( )** alone get reflected back in **main( )**.

From the definitions of each function we can see that each takes different types of arguments, so we may be tempted to overload them. But this is not possible since there is no distinction between call to functions **fun1( )** and **fun3( )**. So, these calls cannot be resolved.

## Challenge 50

Write a program that draws different boxes on the screen by calling the function **drawBox ( r1, c1, r2, c2 )**, where **r1**, **c1** are row, column of top left corner of the box and **r2**, **c2** are row column, of bottom right corner of the box. The four arguments should take default values of 2, 5, 20, 70 respectively.

## Solution

```
// Project: chall50
// Drawing of boxes on screen
#include <iostream>
#include <cstdio>
using namespace std ;

void box ( int sr = 2, int sc = 5, int er = 20, int ec = 70 ) ;
void gotoxy ( short, short ) ;

int main( )
{
    box ( 10, 20, 22, 70 ) ;
    box ( 10, 20, 15 ) ;
    box ( 5, 10 ) ;
    box( ) ;
    return 0 ;
}

void box ( int sr, int sc, int er, int ec )
{
    int r, c ;

    gotoxy ( sc, sr ) ;
    cout << ( char ) 218 ;
    gotoxy ( ec, sr ) ;
    cout << ( char ) 191 ;
    gotoxy ( sc, er ) ;
    cout << ( char ) 192 ;
    gotoxy ( ec, er ) ;
    cout << ( char ) 217 ;

    for ( r = sr + 1 ; r < er ; r++ )
    {
        gotoxy ( sc, r ) ;
```

```
            cout << ( char ) 179 ;
            gotoxy ( ec, r ) ;
            cout << ( char ) 179 ;
        }

        for ( c = sc + 1 ; c < ec ; c++ )
        {
            gotoxy ( c, sr ) ;
            cout << ( char ) 196 ;
            gotoxy ( c, er ) ;
            cout << ( char ) 196 ;
        }
}

void gotoxy ( short col, short row )
{
    printf ( "%c[%d;%df", 0x1B,row,col ) ;
}
```

## Sample Run

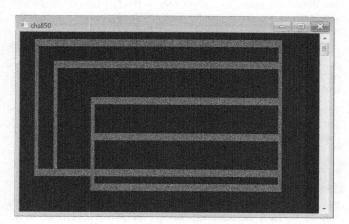

## Explanation

When we call the function **box( )** with 4 arguments the box is drawn with the arguments passed. However, when we call it with 3 arguments the default value mentioned in the prototype of **box( )** is used for the last argument. Likewise, when we call it with two arguments default values are used for the last two arguments, and finally when we call it without any arguments, a box gets drawn with all the four default values mentioned in the prototype. Thus, the default arguments are used if the calling function doesn't supply them when the function is called.

Note that if one argument is missing when the function is called, it is assumed to be the last argument. Thus, the missing arguments must be the trailing arguments (those at the end of the argument list). You can leave out last three arguments, but you cannot leave out the last but one and then put in the last. This is quite reasonable. After all, how would the compiler know which arguments you meant, if you left out some arguments in the middle. Not surprisingly, compiler will flag an error if you leave out some arguments for which the function you are calling doesn't provide default values.

The default arguments are given only in the function prototype and should not be repeated in the function definition. The compiler uses the prototype information to build a call, not the function definition.

The **gotoxy( )** function sends an ANSI sequence to the terminal to position the cursor at desired row and column in the terminal window. An ANSI sequence begins with Esc character whose ASCII value is 27 (0x1B).

To send the output to an external terminal window as shown in the Sample Run, go to project properties and select Run | Console Type | External Terminal.

## Challenge 51

Write a program to track number of objects that are created from a class **Sample**. Define a **showCount( )** member function in it using which we can display at any time the current count of objects that have been created from the **Sample** class.

## Solution

```
// Project: chall51
// Use of static data and static functions
#include <iostream>
using namespace std ;

class Sample
{
    private :

        int i ;
        static int count ;

    public :
        Sample( )
        {
            i = 0 ;
            count++ ;
        }

        static void showCount( )
        {
            cout << "Number of objects: " << count << endl ;
        }
} ;

int Sample :: count = 0 ;

int main( )
{
    Sample s1, s2, s3, s4 ;
    Sample :: showCount( ) ;

    return 0 ;
}
```

## Sample Run

Number of objects: 4

## Explanation

**i** is an instance variable and present in every object, whereas **count** is a static variable, so it is shared amongst all objects. Each time a new object is created in the constructor **i** for that object is initialized to 0, whereas **count**, which is common to all objects is incremented by 1.

**showCount( )** has been marked as a **static** function indicating that it can access only **static** data. It is not called using any object, but by using the special syntax for calling a static function—**classname::functionname( )**. Note that **this** pointer is never passed to a static function.

Also observe the special syntax for initializing a **static** variable outside the class. Had this been done in the constructor, every time an object is created **count** would have been set to 0.

## Challenge 52

Write a program to create **Sample** class as a Singleton class. A Singleton class is a class from which only one object can be created.

## Solution

```
// Project: chall52
// Singleton Class
#include <iostream>
using namespace std ;

class Singleton
{
    private:

        int i ;
        static Singleton *p ;

        Singleton( )
        {
```

```
                i = 0 ;
        }

    public:

        static Singleton* create( )
        {
            if ( p == NULL )
                p = new Singleton ;

            return p ;
        }
} ;

Singleton* Singleton :: p = NULL ;

int main( )
{
    Singleton *s1, *s2, *s3 ;

    s1 = Singleton :: create( ) ;
    s2 = Singleton :: create( ) ;
    s3 = Singleton :: create( ) ;

    cout << s1 << endl ;
    cout << s2 << endl ;
    cout << s3 << endl ;

    return 0 ;
}
```

## Sample Run

```
0x20014c70
0x20014c70
0x20014c70
```

## Explanation

We have declared the constructor of the **Singleton** class as **private**. As a result, it cannot be called from outside the class. Then, we have provided a factory function called **create( )** and marked it as **static**. This means, to call it we do not need an object. We can simply call it using the syntax **Singleton :: create( )**. We have also created a **static** pointer **p** and initialized it to NULL.

In the **create( )** function we have created an object of **Singleton** class only if **p** is NULL. **p** would be NULL when we land into **create( )** for the first time. During subsequent calls to **create( )**, **p** would not be NULL, hence we do not create any additional objects.

## Challenge 53

Suppose there is a class **Sample** which contains a **display( )** function. Two objects **s1** and **s2** are created from the **Sample** class. Using these objects **display( )** function is called. How can it be programmatically proved that each time **display( )** is working on a different object.

## Solution

```cpp
// Project: chall53
// static data and static functions
#include <iostream>
using namespace std ;

class Sample
{
    public :
        void display( )
        {
            cout << "Address of object = " << this << endl ;
        }
} ;

int main( )
{
    Sample s1, s2 ;
    s1.display( ) ;
```

```
    s2.display( ) ;
    return 0 ;
}
```

## Sample Run

Address of object = 0x22cc7f
Address of object = 0x22cc7e

## Explanation

When **display( )** is called using **s1**, address of **s1** is passed to it and when it is called using **s2**, address of **s2** is passed to it. Each time the address is collected in a pointer called **this** pointer. So, when we print the contents of the **this** pointer we get different addresses, proving that each time **display( )** would be working on a different object.

## Challenge 54

Define two inline functions **min( )** and **max( )** that return minimum and maximum of two integers. Are inline functions a good idea?

## Solution

```
// Project: chall54
// Inline functions
#include <iostream>
using namespace std ;

inline int min ( int a, int b )
{
    return ( a < b ) ? a : b ;
}
inline int max ( int a, int b )
{
    return ( a > b ) ? a : b ;
}
int main( )
```

```
{
    cout << min ( 10, 20 ) << endl ;
    cout << max ( -10, -345 ) << endl ;
    return 0 ;
}
```

## Sample Run

```
10
-10
```

## Explanation

**min( )** and **max( )** have been defined as inline functions using the keyword **inline**. Once we declare functions as inline, compiler places a copy of the code of that function at each point where the function is called.

Isn't this similar to macros in C? Yes, but, macros have side-effects, especially when the arguments are expressions. **inline** functions are a solution to these side-effects.

The down side of inline functions is, any change to an inline function could require all clients of the function to be recompiled so that compiler can do the substitutions once again.

Note that the compiler can ignore the inline qualifier in case defined function is complex and big. When we define functions inside a class they are treated as inline functions, even though we do not explicitly specify so.

# 09/ Total Challenges: 5

# Function Overloading Challenges

The function overloading facility in C++ is very useful and avoids defining different function names but essentially carrying out the same job on different data types. This chapter provides challenges that would test your understanding of this useful concept.

163

## Challenge 55

Write a program that contains overloaded functions to find absolute values of different types of arguments passed to them.

## Solution

```
// Project: chall55
// Absolute Value by Function Overloading
#include <iostream>
using namespace std ;

int main( )
{
    int abs ( int ) ;
    long abs ( long ) ;
    double abs ( double ) ;

    int l = -25, x ;
    long m = 1000L, y ;
    double n = 23.65, z ;

    x = abs ( l ) ;
    y = abs ( m ) ;
    z = abs ( n ) ;

    cout << "Absolute value of: " << l << " = " << x << endl ;
    cout << "Absolute value of: " << m << " = " << y << endl ;
    cout << "Absolute value of: " << n << " = " << z << endl ;
}

int abs ( int n )
{
    if ( n >= 0 )
        return n ;
    else
        return ( -1 ) * n ;
}
```

```
long abs ( long n )
{
    if ( n >= 0 )
        return n ;
    else
        return ( -1 ) * n ;
}

double abs ( double n )
{
    if ( n >= 0 )
        return n ;
    else
        return ( -1 ) * n ;
}
```

## Sample Run

```
Absolute value of: -25 = 25
Absolute value of: 1000 = 1000
Absolute value of: 23.65 = 23.65
```

## Explanation

How does the C++ compiler know which of the **abs( )**s should be called when a call is made? It decides that from the type of the argument being passed during the function call. For example, if an **int** is being passed the integer version of **abs( )** gets called, if a **double** is being passed then the double version of **abs( )** gets called and so on. That's quite logical, you would agree.

## Challenge 56

Write a program that contains overloaded function **sort( )** to arrange in ascending order, the integers or doubles passed to it.

## Solution

```
// Project: chall56
// Sorting numbers using overloaded functions
#include <iostream>
using namespace std ;

void sort ( int [ ], int ) ;
void sort ( double [ ], int ) ;

int main( )
{
    int arrint[ ] = {6, 4, 5, 3, 2, 1} ;
    double arrdbl[ ] = {9.2, -8.1, 3.33, 5.2, 6.1, 1.8} ;
    int i ;

    sort ( arrint, 6 ) ;

    for ( i = 0 ; i < 6 ; i++ )
        cout << arrint[ i ] << " " ;
    cout << endl ;

    sort ( arrdbl, 6 ) ;
    for ( i = 0 ; i < 6 ; i++ )
        cout << arrdbl[ i ] << " " ;
    cout << endl ;

    return 0 ;
}

void sort ( int arr[ ], int size )
{
    int i, j, t ;

    for ( i = 0 ; i < size ; i++ )
    {
        for ( j = i + 1 ; j < size ; j++ )
        {
            if ( arr[ i ] > arr[ j ] )
            {
```

```
                    t = arr[ i ] ;
                    arr[ i ] = arr[ j ] ;
                    arr[ j ] = t ;
                }
            }
        }
    }

void sort ( double arr[ ], int size )
{
    int i, j ;
    double t ;

    for ( i = 0 ; i < size ; i++ )
    {
        for ( j = i + 1 ; j < size ; j++ )
        {
            if ( arr[ i ] > arr[ j ] )
            {
                t = arr[ i ] ;
                arr[ i ] = arr[ j ] ;
                arr[ j ] = t ;
            }
        }
    }
}
```

## Sample Run

```
1 2 3 4 5 6
-8.1  1.8  3.33  5.2  6.1  9.2
```

## Explanation

Both versions of the overloaded **sort( )** function implement the Bubble sort algorithm to sort the numbers.

## Challenge  57

Write a program that provides two overloaded **random( )** functions, the first one generates any integer random number, whereas the second generates a random number that lies within the range passed to the **random( )** function.

## Solution

```
// Project: chall57
// Generation of random numbers using overloaded functions
#include <iostream>
using namespace std ;

int random ( int ) ;
int random ( int, int ) ;

int main( )
{
    int i, n ;

    cout << "Random numbers between 1 to 100: " << endl ;
    for ( i = 0 ; i <= 9 ; i++ )
    {
        n = random ( 100 ) ;
        cout << n << endl ;
    }

    cout << "Random numbers between 100 to 500: " << endl ;
    for ( i = 0 ; i <= 9 ; i++ )
    {
        n = random ( 100, 500 ) ;
        cout << n << endl ;
    }
}

int random ( int max )
{
    static int xn = time ( NULL ) % max ;
```

```
        static int cons = time ( NULL ) % 100 ;
        static int mult = time ( NULL ) % 120 ;

        int xnplus1, temp ;

        xnplus1 = ( mult * xn + cons ) % max ;
        temp = xnplus1 ;
        xn = xnplus1 ;

        return ( temp ) ;
}
int random ( int min, int max )
{
        int range ;

        range = max - min ;

        static int xn = time ( NULL ) % range ;
        static int cons = time ( NULL ) % 100 ;
        static int mult = time ( NULL ) % 120 ;
        int xnplus1, temp ;

        xnplus1 = ( mult * xn + cons ) % max ;
        temp = min + xnplus1 ;
        xn = xnplus1 ;

        return ( temp ) ;
}
```

## Sample Run

```
Random numbers between 1 to 100:
72
63
24
55
56
27
68
79
```

60
11
Random numbers between 100 to 500:
572
163
124
355
256
227
168
479
560
311

## Explanation

The program uses a Linear Congruential Generator (LCG) algorithm that yields a sequence of pseudo-random numbers calculated with a discontinuous piecewise linear equation. The generator is defined by the recurrence relation:

$$X_{n+1} = ( a * X_n + c ) \bmod m$$

where **X** is the sequence of pseudorandom values, and

**m** is the modulus with the condition, **0 < m**

**a** is the multiplier with the condition **0 < a < m**

**c** is the increment with the condition $0 <= c < m$

**$X_0$** is the seed value or start value, with the condition **$0 <= X_0 < m$**

## Challenge 58

Write a program that provides overloaded **max( )** function that receives either an array of integers or an array of doubles and returns the maximum value from the array. On similar lines, write the overloaded **min( )** function.

## Solution

```
// Project: chall58
// Overloaded max( ) and min( ) functions
#include <iostream>
using namespace std ;

int min ( int [ ], int, bool* ) ;
double min ( double [ ], int, bool* ) ;

int max ( int [ ], int, bool* ) ;
double max ( double [ ], int, bool* ) ;

int main( )
{
    int arrint[ ] = { 4, 6, 2, 7, 1 } ;
    double arrdbl[ ] = { 6.3, 6.9, 1.4, 5.2, 4.5 } ;

    bool flag = false ;

    int minInt = min ( arrint, 5, &flag ) ;

    if ( flag == true )
        cout << "Invalid size of the array. Unable to find min." << endl ;
    else
        cout << "Minimum of Integer Array: " << minInt << endl ;

    flag = false ;

    double minDouble = min ( arrdbl, 5, &flag ) ;

    if ( flag == true )
        cout << "Invalid size of the array. Unable to find min." << endl ;
    else
        cout << "Minimum of Double Array: " << minDouble << endl ;

    flag = false ;

    int maxInt = max ( arrint, 5, &flag ) ;
```

```cpp
        if ( flag == true )
            cout << "Invalid size of the array. Unable to find max." << endl ;
        else
            cout << "Maximum of Integer Array: " << maxInt << endl ;

        flag = false ;

        double maxDouble = max ( arrdbl, 5, &flag ) ;

        if ( flag == true )
            cout << "Invalid size of the array. Unable to find max." << endl ;
        else
            cout << "Maximum of Double Array: " << maxDouble << endl ;

        return 0 ;
}

int min ( int arr[ ], int size, bool* flag )
{
    if ( size < 1 )
    {
        *flag = true ;
        return -1 ;
    }

    int m = arr[ 0 ] ;
    for ( int i = 1 ; i < size ; i++ )
    {
        if ( arr[ i ] < m )
            m = arr[ i ] ;
    }

    return m ;
}

double min ( double arr[ ], int size, bool* flag )
{
    if ( size < 1 )
    {
        *flag = true ;
        return -1 ;
```

```
    }

    double m = arr[ 0 ] ;
    for ( int i = 1 ; i < size ; i++ )
    {
        if ( arr[ i ] < m )
            m = arr[ i ] ;
    }

    return m ;
}

int max ( int arr[ ], int size, bool* flag )
{
    if ( size < 1 )
    {
        *flag = true ;
        return -1 ;
    }

    int m = arr[ 0 ] ;
    for ( int i = 1 ; i < size ; i++ )
    {
        if ( arr[ i ] > m )
            m = arr[ i ] ;
    }

    return m ;
}

double max ( double arr[ ], int size, bool* flag )
{
    if ( size < 1 )
    {
        *flag = true ;
        return -1 ;
    }

    double m = arr[ 0 ] ;
    for ( int i = 1 ; i < size ; i++ )
    {
```

```
        if ( arr[ i ] > m )
            m = arr[ i ] ;
    }

    return m ;
}
```

## Sample Run

Minimum of Integer Array: 1
Minimum of Double Array: 1.4
Maximum of Integer Array: 7
Maximum of Double Array: 6.9

## Explanation

The program is pretty straight-forward. We have overloaded **max( )** and **min( )** functions to receive arrays of different types and then return maximum or minimum value present in them respectively.

## Challenge   59

Write a program that contains a **Byte** class and overloaded **setBit( )** and **clearBit( )** functions as shown below.

setBit ( num, 3 ) - Sets 1 in bit number 3 in num

setBit ( num, 2, 5 ) - Sets 1 in bits 2 to 5 in num

clearBit ( num, 2 ) - Clears 0 in bit number 2 in num

clearBit ( num, 3, 6 ) - Clears 0 in bits 3 to 6 in num

## Solution

```cpp
// Project: chall59
// Overloaded functions for setting and clearing bits
#include <iostream>
using namespace std ;
```

```
class Byte
{
    private :
        unsigned char ch ;

    public :

        Byte( )
        {
            ch = 0 ;
        }

        Byte ( char c )
        {
            ch = c ;
        }

        void setBit ( int n )
        {
            if ( n >= 0 && n < 8 )
            {
                unsigned char z = 1 ;
                for ( int i = 0 ; i < n ; i++ )
                    z = z << 1 ;

                ch = ch | z ;
            }
            else
                cout << "Index out of range" << endl ;
        }

        void setBit ( int l, int m )
        {
            if ( l >= 0 && l < 8 && m >= 0 && m < 8 && l <= m )
            {
                unsigned char z = 1 ;

                for ( int i = l ; i < m ; i++ )
                {
                    z = z << 1 ;
```

```
            z = z | 1 ;
        }

    for ( int i = 0 ; i < l ; i++ )
        z = z << 1 ;

    ch = ch | z ;
    }
    else
        cout << "Index out of range" << endl ;
}

void clearBit ( int n )
{
    if ( n >= 0 && n < 8 )
    {
        unsigned char z = 1 ;
        for ( int i = 0 ; i < n ; i++ )
            z = z << 1 ;

        z = ~z ;
        ch = ch & z ;
    }
    else
        cout << "Index out of range" << endl ;
}

void clearBit ( int l, int m )
{
    if ( l >= 0 && l < 8 && m >= 0 && m < 8 && l <= m )
    {
        unsigned char z = 1 ;
        for ( int i = l ; i < m ; i++ )
        {
            z = z << 1 ;
            z = z | 1 ;
        }

        for ( int i = 0 ; i < l ; i++ )
            z = z << 1 ;
```

```
                z = ~z ;
                ch = ch & z ;
            }
            else
                cout << "Index out of range" << endl ;
        }

        void displayByte( )
        {
            char i, andmask, k ;

            cout << "Character Value: " ;
            for ( i = 7 ; i >= 0 ; i-- )
            {
                andmask = 1 << i ;
                k = ch & andmask ;
                k == 0 ? cout << "0" : cout << "1" ;
            }
            cout << endl ;
        }
} ;

int main( )
{
    Byte b = Byte ( 'A' ) ;
    cout << "Initial value: " ;
    b.displayByte( ) ;

    b.setBit ( 4 ) ;
    cout << "Value after setting bit number 4: " ;
    b.displayByte( ) ;

    cout << "Value after setting bits 1 to 3: " ;
    b.setBit ( 1, 3 ) ;
    b.displayByte( ) ;

    cout << "Value after clearing bit number 2: " ;
    b.clearBit ( 2 ) ;
    b.displayByte( ) ;

    cout << "Value after clearing bits 4 to 6: " ;
```

```
    b.clearBit ( 4, 6 ) ;
    b.displayByte( ) ;

    return 0 ;
}
```

## Sample Run

Initial value: Character Value: 01000001
Value after setting bit number 4: Character Value: 01010001
Value after setting bits 1 to 3: Character Value: 01011111
Value after clearing bit number 2: Character Value: 01011011
Value after clearing bits 4 to 6: Character Value: 00001011

## Explanation

The program uses bitwise **|** operator to set the bits and **&** operator to clear the bits. Both **setBit( )** and **clearBit( )** have been overloaded to work with either individual bit or a set of bits. Before applying the **|** or **&** operator the mask is built in a variable **z** in all these functions.

# 10 / Total Challenges: 6

# Operator Overloading Challenges

**O**perator overloading is a new feature in C++. It lets you carry out operations on objects of user-defined classes in a manner similar to the operations that you carry out on standard data types. The challenges in this chapter test your comfort level with the operator overloading feature.

## Challenge  60

Write a program to implement an **Index** class, which has a **private int count** in it. It should also have a pre-increment and post-increment overloaded operator in it which increments **count** appropriately.

## Solution

```
// Project: chall60
// Overloading incrementation operator
#include <iostream>
using namespace std ;

class index
{
    private :
        int count ;

    public :

        index( )
        {
            count = 0 ;
        }

        void display( )
        {
            cout << count << endl ;
        }

        index operator ++ ( )
        {
            index t ;
            count++ ;
            t.count = count ;
            return t ;
        }

        index operator ++ ( int n )
```

```
            {
                index t ;
                t.count = count ;
                count++ ;
                return t ;
            }
    } ;

int main( )
{
    index  i, j, k ;

    j = ++i ;
    k = i++ ;
    i.display( ) ;
    j.display( ) ;
    k.display( ) ;
}
```

## Sample Run

2
1
1

## Explanation

We have provided two overloaded operator functions for the **++** operator. The zero-argument version gets called when we pre-increment the **Index** object, as in **j = ++i**. The one-argument version gets called when we post-increment the **Index** object, as in **k = i++**.

The argument **n** in the post-increment version is a dummy argument. Its value is always 0 and is not used in the function definition. It is used only to distinguish between the two functions.

## Challenge   61

Write a program that implements a **Distance** class which records the distance in **meter** and **centimeter**. Overload > and < operator in it which checks whether one **Distance** object is smaller or greater than the other.

## Solution

```
// Project: chall61
// Distance class and operations
#include <iostream>
using namespace std ;

class Distance
{
    private:

        int meter, centimeter ;

    public:

        Distance( )
        {
            meter = 0 ;
            centimeter = 0 ;
        }

        Distance ( int m, int cm )
        {
            meter = m ;
            centimeter = cm ;
        }

        void display( )
        {
            cout << "Distance = " << meter << " m "
                    << centimeter << " cm" <<endl ;
        }

        bool operator < ( const Distance& d )
```

```
            {
                if ( meter < d.meter )
                    return true ;

                if ( meter == d.meter && centimeter < d.centimeter )
                    return true ;

                return false ;
            }


            bool operator > ( const Distance& d )
            {
                if ( meter > d.meter )
                    return true ;

                if ( meter == d.meter && centimeter > d.centimeter )
                    return true ;

                return false ;
            }
    } ;

int main( )
{
    Distance d1 ( 10, 50 ) , d2 ( 15, 30 ) , d3 ( 12, 45 ) ;

    cout << "d1 = " ;
    d1.display( ) ;
    cout << "d2 = " ;
    d2.display( ) ;
    cout << "d3 = " ;
    d3.display( ) ;

    if ( d1 < d2 )
        cout << "d1 is less than d2 " << endl ;
    else
        cout << "d2 is less than d1 " << endl ;

    if ( d1 > d3 )
        cout << "d1 is greater than d3 " << endl ;
```

```
        else
            cout << "d1 is less than d3 " << endl ;

        return 0 ;
}
```

## Sample Run

```
d1 = Distance = 10 m 50 cm
d2 = Distance = 15 m 30 cm
d3 = Distance = 12 m 45 cm
d1 is less than d2
d1 is less than d3
```

## Explanation

The expression **d1 < d2** gets expanded to **d1. operator < ( d2 )**. So in the overloaded operator function when we refer to **meter** and **centimeter** they are **d1's meter** and **centimeter** and when we refer to **d.meter** and **d.centimeter** they are **d2's meter** and **centimeter**.

**d2** is received in the **<** overloaded operator function by reference. This ensures that another copy of **d2** is not made in the function. **const** ensures that we cannot modify **d2** in the overloaded function through **d**.

## Challenge    62

Write a program that implements a **Complex** class to maintain complex numbers. Also provide an overloaded **+** operator in it which can add two complex numbers. Also make a provision to add a complex number with a **double** using the same overloaded operator. In this addition the double value should be taken as the real value of the complex number and imaginary value should be treated as 0.

## Solution

```
// Project: chall62
// Overloading + operator
```

```cpp
#include <iostream>
using namespace std ;

class Complex
{
    private :
        double r, i ;

    public :

        Complex ( double rr = 0, double ii = 0 )
        {
            r = rr ;
            i = ii ;
        }

        void print( )
        {
            cout << r << " " << i << endl ;
        }

        Complex operator + ( Complex x )
        {
            Complex t ;

            t.r = r + x.r ;
            t.i = i + x.i ;

            return t ;
        }
};

int main( )
{
    Complex a ( 1.5, 1.3 ) ;
    Complex b ( 2.5, 2.3 ) ;
    Complex c, d ;

    cout << "a = " ;
    a.print( ) ;
    cout << "b = " ;
```

```
    b.print( ) ;

    c = a + b ;
    cout << "c = " ;
    c.print( ) ;

    double dbl = 1.1 ;
    d = a + dbl ;
    cout << "d = " ;
    d.print( ) ;
}
```

## Sample Run

```
a = 1.5  1.3
b = 2.5  2.3
c = 4  3.6
d = 2.6  1.3
```

## Explanation

The expression **c = a + b** gets expanded to **c = a.operator + ( b )**. So in the overloaded **+** operator function when we refer to **r** and **i** they are **a**'s **r** and **i** and when we refer to **x.r** and **x.i** they are **b**'s **r** and **i**.

When we add **a** with **dbl**, **dbl** is sent to the overloaded operator function, but it is supposed to receive a **Complex**. So there must be a function that can convert a **double** to a **Complex**. This work is done by the constructor. It creates a temporary **Complex** object containing **dbl** value in the real part and 0 in the imaginary part. This temporary object is then passed to the overloaded function which then carries out the addition.

## Challenge    63

In the program in Challenge 62 how the conversion from **double** to **Complex** can be prevented and why would we want to do it?

## Solution

```
// Project: chall63
// Avoiding implicit conversion
 class Complex
{
    private :
        double r, i ;

    public :

        explicit Complex ( double rr = 0, double ii = 0 )
        {
            r = rr ;
            i = ii ;
        }
        // rest of the code would be same as Challenge 62
} ;
```

## Sample Run

Error in the statement d = a + dbl ;

## Explanation

Once we mark the constructor using the **explicit** keyword the implicit conversion of **dbl** into a **Complex** object using the constructor cannot be done. Hence the error.

We marked the constructor as **explicit** because without it the addition **d = a + dbl** works, but the addition **d = dbl + a** would not. This is counter-intuitive, because addition is always supposed to be commutative.

## Challenge 64

Write a program that implements a **Complex** class containing an overloaded **+** operator that can add two **Complex** objects, a **Complex** and a **double**, and a **double** and a **Complex**.

## Solution

```
// Project: chall64
// Overloading using a friend function
#include <iostream>
using namespace std ;

class  Complex
{
    private :
        double  r, i ;

    public :

        Complex ( double rr = 0, double ii = 0 )
        {
            r = rr ;
            i = ii ;
        }

        void print( )
        {
            cout << r << " " << i << endl ;
        }

        friend Complex operator + ( Complex, Complex ) ;
} ;

Complex operator + ( Complex x, Complex y )
{
    Complex  t ;

    t.r = x.r + y.r ;
    t.i = x.i + y.i ;

    return  t ;
}

int main( )
{
```

```
        Complex  a ( 1.5, 1.3 ) ;
        Complex  b ( 2.5, 2.3 ) ;
        Complex  c, d, e ;

        cout << "a = " ;
        a.print( ) ;
        cout << "b = " ;
        b.print( ) ;

        c = a + b ;
        cout << "c = " ;
        c.print( ) ;

        double dbl = 1.1 ;
        d = a + dbl ;
        cout << "d = " ;
        d.print( ) ;

        e = dbl + a ;
        cout << "e = " ;
        e.print( ) ;
}
```

## Sample Run

```
a = 1.5  1.3
b = 2.5  2.3
c = 4  3.6
d = 2.6  1.3
e = 2.6  1.3
```

## Explanation

Here we have declare the overloaded operator **+** function as a **friend** of the class **Complex**. Doing this ensures that the addition **a + dbl** as well as **dbl + a** work, which was not the case earlier when the overloaded function was a **Complex** class member. Secondly, declaring the function as a **friend** of the class ensures that the class's **private** members become accessible to the **friend** function. Note that **this** pointer is never passed to a **friend** function.

## Challenge 65

Write a program that implements a **Complex** class. It should contain <<
and >> overloaded functions to receive or display **Complex** objects.

## Solution

```cpp
// Project: chall65
// Overloading << and >> operators
#include <iostream>
using namespace std ;

class Complex
{
    private :
        double r, i ;

    public :

        Complex ( double rr = 0, double ii = 0 )
        {
            r = rr ;
            i = ii ;
        }

        friend ostream& operator << ( ostream&, Complex ) ;
        friend istream& operator >> ( istream&, Complex& ) ;
} ;

ostream& operator << ( ostream& x, Complex c )
{
    x << c.r << " " << c.i << endl ;
    return x ;
}

istream& operator >> ( istream& x, Complex &c )
{
    x >> c.r >> c.i ;
    return x ;
```

```
}

int main( )
{
    Complex  a, b ;

    cout << "Enter values of a Complex object" << endl ;
    cin >> a ;
    cout << "Enter values of a Complex object" << endl ;
    cin >> b ;
    cout << "Values of a and b are :" << endl ;
    cout << a << b ;
}
```

## Sample Run

```
Enter values of a Complex object
1.1  2.2
Enter values of a Complex object
2.5  4.6
Values of a and b are :
1.1 2.2
2.5 4.6
```

## Explanation

Here we have two **friend** functions. Purpose of **friend** functions is to ensure that to them **private** members of the class in which they are marked as **friend**, are available. Thus both the overloaded operator functions have an access to **r** and **i**, which are **private** members of the **Complex** class.

The **>>** operator receives a **Complex** object by reference, because any changes in this object should be available in **main( )**.

# 11 / Total Challenges: 4

# Free Store Challenges

**F**ree Store means memory. In C++, we can create and delete objects dynamically from memory. This gives flexibility, as we do not have to make a commitment to number of objects that we wish to create. This chapter tests your understanding of this concept and its usage in practice.

## Challenge  66

Write a program that dynamically allocates a 2D integer array of given rows and columns. Populate the array with random numbers. Eliminate the array from memory once its usage is over.

### Solution

```
// Project: chall66
// Dynamically allocated 2D array
#include <iostream>
#include <cstdlib>
#include <ctime>
using namespace std ;

int main( )
{
    const int rows = 4 ;
    const int columns = 5 ;
    int  i, j ;

    // Allocate memory for rows
    int **ptr = new int* [ rows ] ;

    // Now allocate memory for columns
    for ( i = 0 ; i < columns ; i++ )
        ptr[ i ] = new int [ columns ] ;

    time_t t ;
    time ( &t ) ;
    srand ( ( unsigned int ) t ) ;

    for ( i = 0 ; i < rows ; i++ )
    {
        for ( j = 0 ; j < columns ; j++ )
            ptr[ i ][ j ] = rand( ) % 10 ;
    }

    for ( i = 0 ; i < rows ; i++ )
```

```
    {
        for ( j = 0 ; j < columns ; j++ )
            cout << ptr[ i ][ j ] << "\t" ;

        cout << endl ;
    }

    for ( i = 0 ; i < rows ; i++ )
        delete[ ] ptr[ i ] ;

    delete [ ] ptr ;
}
```

## Sample Runs

First run:

| | | | | |
|---|---|---|---|---|
| 4 | 1 | 7 | 8 | 8 |
| 6 | 7 | 0 | 2 | 3 |
| 6 | 4 | 4 | 5 | 2 |
| 1 | 2 | 4 | 3 | 8 |

Second run:

| | | | | |
|---|---|---|---|---|
| 8 | 3 | 4 | 8 | 8 |
| 1 | 5 | 4 | 6 | 4 |
| 9 | 6 | 4 | 6 | 8 |
| 3 | 5 | 7 | 4 | 6 |

## Explanation

Here **ptr** points to an array of pointers. Each element of this array points to a different row of elements in the matrix. All allocation from free store has been done using **new** operator.

Once the 2D array has been allocated, we have populated it with random numbers. Random numbers are generated using the rand( ) function. To ensure that each number stored in the array is a single digit number, we have done mod by 10.

**rand( )** returns random numbers in the same sequence during each execution. To avoid this we have used the system time as a seed for random number generation.

Note that since we have used **new** with **[ ]**, we must de-allocate with **delete** using **[ ]**.

## Challenge 67

Write a program that creates a jagged 2D array of 3 rows dynamically. The number of columns in three rows should be 4, 2 and 5 respectively. Fill the array with random numbers and then free the jagged array.

## Solution

```
// Project: chall67
// Jagged Array
#include <iostream>
#include <cstdlib>
#include <ctime>
using namespace std ;

int main( )
{
    const int rows = 3 ;
    const int cols1 = 4, cols2 = 2, cols3 = 5 ;
    int i, j ;

    // Allocate memory for rows
    int **ptr = new int* [ rows ] ;

    // Now allocate memory for columns
    ptr[ 0 ] = new int[ cols1 ] ;
    ptr[ 1 ] = new int[ cols2 ] ;
    ptr[ 2 ] = new int[ cols3 ] ;

    time_t t ;
    time ( &t ) ;
    srand ( ( unsigned int ) t ) ;
```

```
    for ( j = 0 ; j < cols1 ; j++ )
        ptr[ 0 ][ j ] = rand( ) % 10 ;

    for ( j = 0 ; j < cols2 ; j++ )
        ptr[ 1 ][ j ] = rand( ) % 10 ;

    for ( j = 0 ; j < cols3 ; j++ )
        ptr[ 2 ][ j ] = rand( ) % 10 ;

    for ( j = 0 ; j < cols1 ; j++ )
        cout << ptr[ 0 ][ j ] << "\t" ;

    cout << endl ;

    for ( j = 0 ; j < cols2 ; j++ )
        cout << ptr[ 1 ][ j ] << "\t" ;

    cout << endl ;

    for ( j = 0 ; j < cols3 ; j++ )
        cout << ptr[ 2 ][ j ] << "\t" ;

    cout << endl ;

    for ( i = 0 ; i < rows ; i++ )
        delete[ ] ptr[ i ] ;

    delete [ ] ptr ;
}
```

## Sample Runs

First run:

```
2    4    1    4
9    4
6    9    4    6    0
```

Second run:

```
3    4    0    4
```

```
9    4
5    6    5    1    1
```

## Explanation

This program is similar to the one in Challenge 67, the only difference being we allocate space each row separately. This is necessary since each row contains different number of elements.

## Challenge  68

Write a program that implements a **Sample** class that has an **int** pointer and a **float** pointer as its **private** data members. While creating objects of this class, in the constructor, allocate space for the integer and the float and set them up with some values. Ensure that the objects are destroyed systematically.

## Solution

```cpp
// Project: chall68
// Avoid memory leaks
#include <iostream>
using namespace std ;

class ex
{
    private :

        int *p ;
        float *q ;

    public :

        ex ( int ii, float aa )
        {
            p = new int ;
            q = new float ;
            *p = ii ;
```

```
            *q = aa ;
        }

        ~ex( )
        {
            delete p ;
            delete q ;
        }

        void display( )
        {
            cout << *p << "\t" << *q << endl ;
        }
} ;

int main( )
{
    ex e1 ( 10, 5.5 ) ;
    e1.display( ) ;
    ex e2 ( 20, 2.4 ) ;
    e2.display( ) ;
}
```

## Sample Run

```
10    5.5
20    2.4
```

## Explanation

When objects **e1** and **e2** die, for each one of them, the destructor gets called. In the destructor, using **delete** we have deleted the **int** and **float** that **p** and **q** are pointing to. If we do not do this, a memory leak would occur.

## Challenge   69

Is **new** same as **malloc( )** and is **delete** same as **free( )**?

## Explanation

No. They are similar, not same. **malloc( )** merely allocates memory and **free( )** releases it. As against this, **new** allocates memory and calls constructor, whereas **delete** calls destructor and de-allocates memory.

The call to the constructor ensures that the object is properly initialized, whereas the call to the destructor ensures that the object is properly destroyed without causing any memory leaks.

**malloc( )** and **free( )** should be used in a C program because in C there is no concept of objects, constructors or destructors. **new** and **delete** should be used in a C++ program. Note that **malloc( )** and **free( )** are not compatible with **new** and **delete**. This means don't allocate using **malloc( )** and release using **delete**, or don't allocate using **new** and release using **free( )**.

# 12 / Total Challenges: 5

# Inheritance Challenges

Inheritance is one of the very important code reuse mechanisms available in C++. It permits us to reuse classes and add / modify their functionality even if their source code is not available. This chapter poses several challenges that test your understanding of this very important concept of OOP.

## Challenge  70

Write a program that has an **Index** class in it that keeps a **count** that gets incremented when **++** is done on an **Index** object. Derive from it an **Index1** class, which provides the overloaded decrementation operator.

### Solution

```
// Project: chall70
// Inheritance demo
#include <iostream>
using namespace std ;

class Index
{
    protected :
        int count ;

    public :

        Index( )
        {
            count = 0 ;
        }

        void display( )
        {
            cout << "Current value of count = " << count << endl ;
        }

        void operator ++ ( )
        {
            count++ ;
        }
} ;

class Index1 : public Index
{
    public :
```

```
        void operator -- ( )
        {
            count-- ;
        }
} ;

int main( )
{
    Index1 j ;

    j.display( ) ;
    ++j ;
    j.display( ) ;
    ++j ;
    j.display( ) ;
    --j ;
    j.display( ) ;
}
```

## Sample Run

```
Current value of count = 0
Current value of count = 1
Current value of count = 2
Current value of count = 1
```

## Explanation

To make count available in the derived class we must declare it as protected. When **display( )** or **++ ( )** are called using **j,** they are first searched in **Index1** class. Since they are not found there, the search proceeds to the base class i.e. the **Index** class. Since these functions are found in **Index** class, they are executed from there. As against this, when **-- ( )** is called, it is searched in **Index1** class and since it is found in **Index1**, it is executed from **Index1**.

## Challenge 71

Write a program that displays the sequence of calling constructors during inheritance.

## Solution

```
// Project: chall71
// Constructor inheritance
#include <iostream>
using namespace std ;

class Sample
{
    protected :
        int count ;

    public :

        Sample( )
        {
            count = 0 ;
            cout << "Reached 0-arg Ctor of Sample" << endl ;
        }

        Sample ( int k )
        {
            count = k ;
            cout << "Reached 1-arg Ctor of Sample" << endl ;
        }
} ;

class NewSample : public Sample
{
    private :
        int newcount ;

    public :
```

```
            NewSample( )
            {
                newcount = count * 20 ;
                cout << "Reached 0-arg Ctor of NewSample" << endl ;
            }

            NewSample ( int k ) : Sample ( k )
            {
                newcount = count * 20 ;
                cout << "Reached 1-arg Ctor of NewSample" << endl ;
            }
} ;

int main( )
{
    cout << "Ctor calling order for i :" << endl ;
    Sample i ;

    cout << "Ctor calling order for j :" << endl ;
    NewSample j ;

    cout << "Ctor calling order for k :" << endl ;
    NewSample k ( 30 ) ;
}
```

## Sample Run

```
Ctor calling order for i :
Reached 0-arg Ctor of Sample
Ctor calling order for j :
Reached 0-arg Ctor of Sample
Reached 0-arg Ctor of NewSample
Ctor calling order for k :
Reached 1-arg Ctor of Sample
Reached 1-arg Ctor of NewSample
```

## Explanation

When we create an object of derived class, unlike normal member
functions, constructors of base class as well as derived class get called, in

that sequence. This order of calling is important. While constructing **j**, it is necessary that **count** gets set up properly, otherwise **newcount** cannot be set properly, as it depends on correct value of **count**. Note the syntax used in calling one-argument constructor of the base class.

Had we not called the one-argument constructor of the base class explicitly, then, the zero-argument constructor of base class would have been called.

## Challenge  72

What purpose does inheritance serve?

## Explanation

Inheritance is a code reuse mechanism that lets us reuse existing classes even when their object code alone is available (i.e. when their source code is not available). It is commonly used to implement following functionalities:

(a)   To use existing features of a base class as it is

(b)   To modify an existing functionality of the base class

(c)   To provide additional new functionality through the derived class

(d)   To make a combination of the old functionality from base class and new functionality from derived class.

## Challenge  73

Write a program that throws light on object sizes in multi-level inheritance.

## Solution

```
// Project: chall73
// Multi-level inheritance
```

```
#include <iostream>
using namespace std ;

class Sample
{
    private : int a ;
    protected : int b ;
    public : int c ;
} ;

class NewSample : public Sample
{
    private : int i ;
    protected : int j ;
    public : int k ;
} ;

class FreshSample : public NewSample
{
    private : int x ;
    protected : int y ;
    public : int z ;
} ;

int main( )
{
    Sample s1 ;
    NewSample s2 ;
    FreshSample s3 ;

    cout << "Size of s1 = " << sizeof ( s1 ) << endl ;
    cout << "Size of s2 = " << sizeof ( s2 ) << endl ;
    cout << "Size of s3 = " << sizeof ( s3 ) << endl ;
}
```

## Sample Run

Size of s1 = 12
Size of s2 = 24
Size of s3 = 36

## Explanation

Size of an object is equal to sum of sizes of all its data members plus the sum of sizes of data members in its base class. So **i** being **private**, it is not available to class **NewSample**, but being available or not has got nothing to do with the size of the object. Likewise, **i** and **x** are not available to **FreshSample**, but they are very much a part of object **s3**.

## Challenge 74

Write a program that has 3 classes in it—**Shape**, **Cost** and **Rectangle**. Of these, **Shape** and **Cost** should be independent classes, whereas **Rectangle** should be derived from **Shape** and **Cost**. **Shape** should maintain shape type (Plate or Ring) and length and breadth of the plate/ring. The **Cost** class should have a **getCost( )** function which would return the cost of polishing the shape based on the type of the shape. The **Rectangle** class should contain a function **getQuantity( )** that returns the area if the shape type is a plate and perimeter if the shape type is a rectangular ring. Create objects of the **Rectangle** class in **main( )** and call **getQuantity( )** and **getCost( )** using these objects to determine the quantity and polishing each.

## Solution

```
// Project: chall74
// Multiple inheritance
#include <iostream>
using namespace std ;

enum ShapeType { plate, ring } ;

class Shape
{
    protected :

        ShapeType st ;
        int lrec, brec ;
```

```
        public :
            void setData ( ShapeType s, int l, int b )
            {
                st = s ;
                lrec = l ;
                brec = b ;
            }
} ;

class Cost
{
    public :
        int getCost ( ShapeType st, int qty )
        {
            if ( st == plate )
                return qty * 50 ;
            else
                return qty * 22 ;
        }
} ;

class Rectangle: public Shape, public Cost
{
    public :

        int getQuantity( )
        {
            int qty ;

            if ( st == plate )
                qty = lrec * brec ;
            else
                qty = 2 * ( lrec + brec ) ;
        }
} ;

int main( )
{
    int shint, l, b, qty, cost ;
    ShapeType st ;
    Rectangle r1, r2 ;
```

```
        cout << "Enter shape type: ( 0 - Plate, 1 - Ring ) " << endl ;
        cin >> shint ;
        if ( shint == 0 )
            st = plate ;
        else
            st = ring ;

        cout << "Enter length and breadth of rectangle: " << endl ;
        cin >> l >> b ;

        r1.setData ( st, l, b ) ;
        qty = r1.getQuantity( ) ;
        cost = r1.getCost ( st, qty ) ;
        cout << "Quantity :" << qty << " Cost = " << cost << endl ;

        r2.setData ( ring, 15, 75 ) ;
        qty = r2.getQuantity( ) ;
        cost = r2.getCost ( st, qty ) ;
        cout << "Quantity = " << qty << " Cost = " << cost << endl ;

        return 0 ;
}
```

## Sample Run

```
Enter shape type: (0 - Plate, 1 - Ring)
0
Enter length and breadth of rectangle:
10 20
Quantity = 200 Cost = 10000
Quantity = 180 Cost = 9000
```

## Explanation

The program uses multiple inheritance to derive **Rectangle** class from two base classes—**Shape** and **Cost**. Note that we need to mark **ShapeType**, **lrec** and **brec** as **protected** to make them available to the derived class. Also note that **ShapeType** is not available to the base class **Cost** and has to be explicitly passed to **getCost( )**.

# 13 / Total Challenges: 5

# Virtual Function Challenges

**R**untime polymorphism is perhaps the hardest concept that one encounters while learning C++ programming. It is facilitated through virtual functions. This chapter poses challenges your understanding of this wonderful concept.

## Challenge  75

Write a program to create a **Shape** class containing a pure virtual **draw( )** function. Inherit from this two classes—**Rectangle** and **Circle**. Create an array of upcasted pointers in **main( )** and call the **draw( )** function using its elements. Each call should take control to appropriate class' **draw( )** function.

## Solution

```
// Project: chall75
// Virtual function calls
#include <iostream>
using namespace std ;

class  Shape
{
    public :
        virtual void draw( ) = 0 ;
} ;

class  Circle : public  Shape
{
    public :
        void draw( )
        {
            cout << "In Circle class's draw" << endl ;
        }
} ;

class Rectangle : public Shape
{
    public :
        void draw( )
        {
            cout << "In Rectangle class's draw" << endl ;
        }
} ;
```

```
int main( )
{
    Circle  c1, c2, c3, c4, c5 ;
    Rectangle  r1, r2, r3, r4, r5 ;
    Shape  *p[ ] = { &r1, &c1, &r2, &c2, &r3, &c3, &r4, &c4, &r5, &c5 } ;
    int i ;

    for ( i = 0 ; i < 10 ; i++ )
        p[ i ] -> draw( ) ;
}
```

## Sample Run

In Rectangle class's draw
In Circle class's draw
In Rectangle class's draw
In Circle class's draw
In Rectangle class's draw
In Circle class's draw
In Rectangle class's draw
In Circle class's draw
In Rectangle class's draw
In Circle class's draw

## Explanation

Here, **Shape** is an abstract class. We cannot create objects from this class. **p** is an array of upcasted pointers containing addresses of several **Rectangle** and **Circle** objects. In the loop, when we call **draw( )**, depending on whose address is stored in **p[ i ]**, that class's **draw( )** gets called.

## Challenge 76

How is polymorphism using virtual functions different than compile-time polymorphism?

## Explanation

The term binding refers to the connection between a function call and the actual code executed as a result of the call. If the function invoked in response to each call is known at compile-time, it is called static or early binding, because the compiler can figure out the function to be called before the program is run.

When virtual functions are called using pointer it is known as dynamic binding. Dynamic binding is so named because the actual function called at run-time depends on the contents of the pointer. It is also known as late binding, because the connection between the function call and the actual code executed by the call is determined late during the execution of the program and not when the program is compiled.

The keyword virtual tells the compiler that it should not perform early binding. Instead, it should automatically install all the mechanisms necessary to perform late binding.

## Challenge  77

What are the basic requirements to be met for runtime polymorphism to work?

## Explanation

Following are the requirements that should be met for runtime polymorphism:

(a) There must be inheritance.

(b) The function names in the base and derived class must be same.

(c) Function must be marked as virtual in the base class.

(d) The call to the function must happen through a pointer (upcasted or not).

## Challenge 78

What are VTABLE and VPTRs? How do they work?

### Explanation

To accomplish late binding, the compiler creates a table called VTABLE for each class that contains virtual functions and for the classes derived from it. The compiler places the addresses of the virtual functions for that particular class in the VTABLE. If you don't redefine a function that was declared virtual in the base class, the compiler uses the address of the base-class version in the derived class's VTABLE.

The compiler inserts a pointer called VPTR in every object that is created from a class that has one or more virtual functions in it. When objects of the base class are created the VPTR in them point to base class's VTABLE. When objects of derived class are created the VPTR in them point to derived class's VTABLE.

When we call a virtual function through a pointer the compiler quietly inserts code to fetch the VPTR present in the object whose address is present in the pointer and look up the virtual function's address in the VTABLE, thus calling the right function and causing late binding to take place.

All of this—setting up the VTABLE for each class, initializing the VPTR, inserting the code for the virtual function call—happens automatically, so you don't have to worry about it.

## Challenge 79

Write a program that convincingly illustrates that a virtual function cannot be early bound.

### Solution

```
// Project: chall79
```

```cpp
// Virtual function binding
#include <iostream>
using namespace std ;

class Shape
{
    public :
        virtual void draw( )
        {
            cout << "In Shape class's draw" << endl ;
        }
} ;

class Circle : public Shape
{
    public :
        void draw( )
        {
            cout << "In Circle class's draw" << endl ;
        }
} ;

void fun ( Shape *p ) ;

int main( )
{
    Shape q ;
    Circle c ;
    int num ;

    cout << "Enter 1 for Shape, 2 for Circle: " ;
    cin >> num ;

    if ( num == 1 )
        fun ( &q ) ;
    else
        fun ( &c ) ;
}

void fun ( Shape *p )
{
```

```
    p -> draw( ) ;
}
```

## Sample Runs

Enter 1 for Shape, 2 for Circle: 1
In Shape class's draw
Enter 1 for Shape, 2 for Circle: 2
In Circle class's draw

## Explanation

Here the call **p->draw( )** cannot be early bound because what would **p** contain cannot be determined at compile time. This is because we get to supply the value to **num** only at execution time. And based on the value present in **num** we either pass **Shape** object's address or **Circle** object's address to **fun( )**. And during runtime, based on which object's address is received in **p**, the appropriate class's **draw( )** function is called, as can be seen from the output shown in sample runs.

# 14 / Total Challenges: 6

# Input / Output Challenges

There is no use of a program that tells the secrets to itself. Ultimately all programs have to communicate with the outside world through the Input / Output facilities provided by a language. This chapter tests your understanding of I/O facilities provided in C++.

YASHAVANT & ADITYA KANETKAR'S

## 101 Challenges
### In C++ Programming

Solve 101 Challenges to hone C++ Programming skills
Practise them to be a mature C++ programmer

219

## Challenge 80

Write a program that demonstrates the use of **ios** formatting flags for floating-point precision, the output field width, padding character etc.

### Solution

```
// Project: chall80
// ios formatting flags
#include <iostream>
#include <iomanip>
using namespace std ;

int main( )
{
    int i = 52 ;
    float a = 425.0 ;
    float b = 123.500328 ;
    char str[ ] = "Dream. Then make it happen!" ;

    cout.setf ( ios::unitbuf ) ;

    cout.setf ( ios::showpos ) ;
    cout << i << endl ;

    cout.setf ( ios::showbase ) ;
    cout.setf ( ios::uppercase ) ;
    cout.setf ( ios::hex, ios::basefield ) ;
    cout << i << endl ;

    cout.setf ( ios::oct, ios::basefield ) ;
    cout << i << endl ;

    cout.fill ( '0' ) ;
    cout << "Fill character: " << cout.fill( ) << endl ;

    cout.setf ( ios::dec, ios::basefield ) ;
    cout.width ( 10 ) ;
    cout << i << endl ;
```

```
cout.setf ( ios::left, ios::adjustfield ) ;
cout.width ( 10 ) ;
cout << i << endl ;

cout.setf ( ios::internal, ios::adjustfield ) ;
cout.width ( 10 ) ;
cout << i << endl ;
cout << i << endl ; // without width ( 10 )

cout.width ( 10 ) ;
cout << str << endl ;
cout.width ( 40 ) ;
cout << str << endl ;
cout.setf ( ios::left, ios::adjustfield ) ;
cout.width ( 40 ) ;
cout << str << endl ;

cout.precision ( 6 ) ;
cout << "Precision: " << cout.precision( ) ;
cout.setf ( ios::showpoint ) ;
cout.unsetf ( ios::showpos ) ;
cout << endl << a ;
cout.unsetf ( ios::showpoint ) ;
cout << endl << a ;

cout.setf ( ios::fixed, ios::floatfield ) ;
cout << endl << b ;
cout.setf ( ios::scientific, ios::floatfield ) ;
cout << endl << b ;

b = 5.375 ;
cout.precision ( 14 ) ;
cout.setf ( ios::fixed, ios::floatfield ) ;
cout << endl << b ;
cout.setf ( ios::scientific, ios::floatfield ) ;
cout << endl << b << endl ;

cout.unsetf ( ios::showpoint ) ;
cout.unsetf ( ios::unitbuf ) ;

return 0 ;
```

```
}
```

## Sample Run

```
+52
0X34
064
Fill character: 0
0000000+52
+520000000
+000000052
+52
Dream. Then make it happen!
0000000000000Dream. Then make it happen!
Dream. Then make it happen!0000000000000
Precision: +6
425.000
425
123.500328
1.235003E+02
5.37500000000000
5.37500000000000E+00
```

## Explanation

The on/off flags are simple. They can be turned on through the **setf( )** function and off through the **unsetf( )** function.

The flags that can be set/unset in this manner include **skipws**, **showbase**, **showpoint**, **uppercase**, **showpos**, **unitbuf** and **stdio**.

The second type of formatting flags work in a group. You can have only one of these flags on at a time. To set these flags, you must use the second form of **setf( )** function. For example, there's a flag for each of the number bases: hexadecimal, decimal, and octal. Collectively, these flags are referred to as the **ios::basefield**. If the **ios::dec** flag is set and you call **setf ( ios::hex )**, you'll set the **ios::hex** flag, but you won't clear the **ios::dec** bit, resulting in undefined behavior. The proper thing to do is call the another form of **setf( )** like this:

cout.setf ( ios::hex, ios::basefield ) ;

This call first clears all the bits in the **ios::basefield**, then sets **ios::hex**.

Similarly, the flags **scientific** and **fixed** are referred to as **ios::floatfield**. Also, the flags **left**, **right** and **internal** are collectively referred as **ios::adjustfield**.

There are data members in the **ios** class that control the width of the output field, the fill character used when the data doesn't fill the output field, and the precision for printing floating-point numbers. The values of these variables can be read and written by member functions of the same name.

A small note about the field width values—when the specified width is less than the number of characters that represent the value the specified width is ignored. Thus, if you try to print 412 with a width of two, you'll still get 412. The field width specifies a minimum number of characters; there's no way to specify a maximum number.

Also, the width is reset to zero by each insertion and extraction. If we want to have a constant width, we need to call **width( )** after each insertion or extraction.

Most of the output is self-explanatory. The **unitbuf** and **stdio** flag deserve some explanation. The unit buffering should be turned on when we want to ensure that each character is output as soon as it is inserted into an output stream. You can also use unbuffered output, but unit buffering provides better performance.

## Challenge 81

Write a program using manipulators to produce similar output as in Challenge 80.

## Solution

```
// Project: chall81
// Standard manipulators usage
#include <iostream>
#include <iomanip>
using namespace std ;
```

```cpp
int main( )
{
    int i = 52 ;
    float a = 425.0 ;
    float b = 123.500328f ;
    char str[ ] = "Dream. Then make it happen!" ;

    cout << setiosflags ( ios::unitbuf | ios::showpos ) ;
    cout << i << endl ;

    cout << setiosflags ( ios::showbase | ios::uppercase ) ;
    cout << hex << i << endl ;

    cout << oct << i << endl ;

    cout << setfill ( '0' ) ;
    cout << "Fill character:" << cout.fill( ) << endl ;

    cout << dec << setw ( 10 ) << i << endl ;
    cout << setiosflags ( ios::left )
        << dec << setw ( 10 ) << i << endl ;

    cout << setiosflags ( ios::internal )
        << dec << setw ( 10 ) << i << endl ;
    cout << i << endl ;

    cout << setw ( 10 ) << str << endl ;
    cout << setw ( 40 ) << str << endl ;
    cout << setiosflags ( ios::left ) << setw ( 40 ) << str << endl ;

    cout.precision ( 6 ) ;
    cout << "Precision: " << cout.precision( ) ;
    cout << setiosflags ( ios::showpoint ) << resetiosflags ( ios::showpos )
        << endl << a ;
    cout << resetiosflags ( ios::showpoint )
        << endl << a ;

    cout << setiosflags ( ios::fixed ) << endl << b ;
    cout << resetiosflags ( ios::showpoint | ios::unitbuf ) << endl ;

    return 0 ;
```

```
}
```

```
+52
0X34
064
Fill character:0
0000000+52
+520000000
0000000+52
+52
Dream. Then make it happen!
0000000000000Dream. Then make it happen!
0000000000000Dream. Then make it happen!
Precision: +6
425.000
425
123.500328
```

## Explanation

Calling the member functions of the **ios** class to set the formatting data of the stream is a little tedious. The actions of these functions can be more easily (and cleanly) duplicated using manipulators. When we use manipulators the formatting instructions are inserted directly into a stream.

Manipulators come in two flavors: those that take an argument and those that don't. Manipulators with no arguments are provided in 'iostream', whereas those that take arguments are provided in 'iomanip'. Figure 14.1 gives a list of all manipulators along with their function.

| Manipulator | Purpose |
|---|---|
| skipws | Skip whitespace on input |
| noskipws | Do not skip whitespace on input |
| dec | Convert to decimal |
| oct | Convert to octal |
| hex | Convert to hexadecimal |
| left | Left align, pad on right |
| right | Right align, pad on left |
| internal | Use padding between sign and value |
| endl | Insert newline and flush the output stream |
| showpos | Shows plus sign for positive values |
| noshowpos | Do not show plus sign for positive values |
| uppercase | Display uppercase A-F for hex values, and E for scientific values |
| nouppercase | Do not display hex values in uppercase |
| showpoint | Show decimal point and trailing zeros for float values |
| noshowpoint | Do not show decimal point & trailing zeros for float values |
| scientific | Use scientific notation for printing float values |
| fixed | Use fixed notation for printing float values |
| ends | Insert null character to terminate an output string |
| flush | Flush the output stream |
| lock | Lock file handle |
| unlock | Unlock file handle |
| setw ( int n ) | Changes the field width for output to *n* |
| setfill ( char n ) | Changes fill character to *n* (default - space) |
| setprecision ( int n ) | Changes the precision to *n* places after decimal point |
| setbase ( base n ) | Changes base to *n*, where *n* is 8, 10 or 16 |
| setiosflags ( fmtflags n ) | Sets format flags specified by *n*. Setting remains in effect until next change |
| resetiosflags ( fmtflags n ) | Clears only the format flags specified by *n*. Setting remains in effect until next change |

Figure 14.1

## Challenge 82

Write a program to create two user-defined manipulators called **tab** and **roman**. The tab manipulator should output a '\t' to the output stream and the **roman** manipulator should receive a roman **string** as an argument and send its decimal equivalent to the output stream.

## Solution

```
// Project: chall82
// User-defined manipulators
#include <iostream>
using namespace std ;

ostream& tab ( ostream& o )
{
    return o << "\t" ;
}

class roman
{
    private :

        string str ;

    public :

        roman ( string s )
        {
            str = s ;
        }

        friend ostream& operator << ( ostream&, const roman& ) ;
} ;

ostream& operator << ( ostream& o, const roman& r )
{

    struct key
```

```cpp
{
    char ch ;
    int val ;
} ;

key z[ ] = {
                {'m', 1000},
                {'d', 500},
                {'c', 100},
                {'l', 50},
                {'x', 10},
                {'v', 5},
                {'i', 1}
            } ;

int num = 0 ;
int prev ;
int sz = sizeof ( z ) / sizeof ( z[ 0 ] ) ;

for ( int i = 0 ; i < r.str.length ( ) ; i++ )
{
    int j ;

    for ( j = 0 ; j < sz ; j++ )
    {
        if ( z[ j ].ch == r.str[ i ] )
        {
            break ;
        }
    }

    num = num + z[ j ].val ;
    if ( i != 0 && prev < z[ j ].val )
        num = num - 2 * prev ;

    prev = z[ j ].val ;
}

o << num ;

return o ;
```

```
}

int main( )
{
    string str1 = "viii" ;
    string str2 = "mcmxcviii" ;

    cout << "Roman: " << str1 << tab << "Dec: " << roman ( str1 ) << endl;
    cout << "Roman: " << str2 << tab << "Dec: " << roman ( str2 ) << endl;

    return 0 ;
}
```

## Sample Run

```
Roman: viii    Dec: 8
Roman: mcmxcviii    Dec: 1998
```

## Explanation

To understand how to develop a zero-argument manipulator we need to understand the internal working of some existing manipulator, say **endl**. **endl** is simply a function that take as its argument an **ostream** reference. The declaration for **endl( )** in 'iostream' looks like this.

ostream& endl ( ostream& ) ;

Consider the statement

cout << endl ;

Since << is an overloaded operator, internally this statement becomes,

cout.operator << ( endl ) ;

**endl( )** being a function what is being passed to the overloaded operator is a pointer to a function. The << operator has been defined in 'iostream' as follows:

```
ostream & ostream::operator << ( ostream & ( *_f ) (ostream & ) )
{
```

```
    return ( *_f )( *this ) ;
}
```

This indicates that when we pass the address of **endl( )** to this function it collects it in a pointer to a function that receives an **ostream** reference and returns an **ostream** reference. If you observe carefully this matches the prototype of the **endl( )** function. Since this operator function is called through the **cout** object the **this** pointer contains the address of **cout**. Hence **\*this** yields the object. This object is then passed to the **endl( )** function through the statement.

( *_f )( *this ) ;

On getting called all that the **endl( )** function does is emit a '\n' to the output stream.

Our user-defined **tab( )** manipulator function works exactly same as **endl( )**, except that it emits a '\t' instead of a '\n'.

To implement this **roman( )** manipulator we need to define a class called **roman**. This class consists of a constructor and an overloaded << operator function.

Observe the following statement carefully:

cout << roman ( str1 ) ;

Here **roman ( str1 )** creates a temporary object of the type **roman**. Naturally, while creating this temporary object the constructor gets called and the value passed to it gets set in the **private** variable **str**. This temporary object and the **cout** object are then passed to the overloaded **operator << ( )** function. Note that in case of a **friend** the call to the operator function *doesn't* get converted into the form

cout.operator << ( roman ( str1 ) ) ;

Within the operator function we have converted the value in **str** into its decimal equivalent and outputted it using the reference of the **cout** object. In the end, we have returned the reference. This returning of reference is necessary if we are to use the manipulator in a cascaded **cout**.

## Challenge 83

Write a program to write numeric and string data into a file. Read the same file back and display the contents read on the screen.

## Solution

```
// Project: chall83
// File IO of numeric and string data
#include <fstream>
#include <iostream>
using namespace std ;

int main( )
{
    // create file for output
    ofstream outfile ( "SAMPLE.TXT" ) ;

    char ch = 'Z' ;
    int i = 25 ;
    float a = 473.14f ;
    char str[ ] = "Hyperbole!" ;

    // send data to file
    outfile << ch << endl << i << endl << a << endl << str ;

    outfile.close( ) ;

    ifstream infile ( "SAMPLE.TXT" ) ;

    // read data from file
    infile >> ch >> i >> a >> str ;

    // send data to screen
    cout << ch << endl << i << endl << a << endl << str << endl ;

    return 0 ;
}
```

## Sample Run

25
473.14
Hyperbole!

## Explanation

To begin with, we have defined an object called **outfile** of type **ofstream** class through the statement

ofstream outfile ( "SAMPLE.TXT" ) ;

This invokes the one argument constructor of the **ofstream** class. This constructor allocates resources and opens the file SAMPLE.TXT. But we didn't mention whether the file is to be opened for reading or writing. This is not necessary since the constructor uses the defaults. The prototype of the constructor looks like this.

ofstream ( const char*, int = ios::out, int = filebuf::openprot ) ;

When we do not pass the second parameter to this constructor it uses the **ios::out** as the default file opening mode. Hence the file gets opened for writing.

The third parameter corresponds to the access permission, and it is used unless **ios::nocreate** is specified in the file opening mode. The default value is set to read and write permission.

Sometimes, we may not know the name of the file when the **ofstream** object is created. In such a case we may first create the object and then call **ofstream::open( )** function to open the file as shown below.

ofstream outfile ;
outfile.open ( "SAMPLE.TXT" ) ;

Once again we have not mentioned the file opening mode. The reason is same—**ios::out** has been binarily included (ORed) into the mode (second parameter).

Later, when the file is opened for reading once again a one-argument constructor of **ifstream** class is invoked. This constructor uses the **ios::in** by default to open the file for input.

The insertion operator << has been appropriately overloaded in the **ostream** class (from which **ofstream** is derived) to write different data types to the relevant stream. We can use the same operator functions to output data to the file. This we have done through the statement

outfile << ch << endl << i << endl << a << endl << str ;

Note that while writing this data we have separated each data item from the other using a newline. This is necessary because when we attempt to write numbers like 25 and 473.14 they are written as numeric strings. That is, 473.14 is written as '4', '7', '3', '.', '1', '4'.

For reading the data back we have built an object of the **istream** class. Constructor of this object opens the 'SAMPLE.TXT' file for reading. Once opened, we have used the overloaded extraction operator of the class **istream** to read the data from the file. The '\n' written at the end of every data item helps the overloaded operator to distinguish the various items. When the numeric strings are read back from the file they are converted back to their binary representation for storage in program variables.

We have specifically closed the file once writing is over by calling the function **ostream::close( )**. This is necessary since we wanted to open the same file for reading.

Note that we didn't close the file once reading from the file was over. This is because on termination of the program the **infile** object goes out of scope. As a result, the destructor gets called which closes the file.

The **ifstream**, **ofstream**, and **fstream** classes are declared in the header file '**fstream**'. This file also includes the '**iostream**' header file, so there is no need to include it explicitly.

## Challenge 84

Write a program to write strings into a file. Read the same file back and display the contents read on the screen.

## Solution

// Project: chall84
// String IO

```
#include <fstream>
#include <iostream>
using namespace std ;

int main( )
{
    // create file for output
    ofstream outfile ( "SAMPLE.TXT" ) ;

    // send text to file
    outfile << "You should be enthusiastic about your future\n" ;
    outfile << "That is where you are going to spend the rest of
                    your life\n" ;

    outfile.close( ) ;

    const int MAX = 100 ;
    char str[ MAX ] ;

    // create file for input
    ifstream infile ( "SAMPLE.TXT" ) ;

    // so long as end of file is not encountered
    while ( !infile.eof( ) )
    {
        // read a line of text
        infile.getline ( str, MAX ) ;

        // display the text read from the file
        cout << endl << str ;
    }

    return 0 ;
}
```

## Sample Run

You should be enthusiastic about your future
That is where you are going to spend the rest of your life

## Explanation

Here, we have read the text from the file one line at a time using the **getline( )** function. This function is a member of **istream** (from which **ifstream** is derived). It reads characters until it encounters the end of line character, '\n', and places the resulting string in the buffer **str** supplied as an argument. The maximum size of the buffer is given as the second argument. The contents of the buffer are displayed after each line is read. This goes on till all the lines have been read.

Within the **while** loop we keep checking whether we are through with reading the entire contents of the file. For this we have called the function **ifstream::eof( )**. This function returns a value zero if the end of file is reached, non-zero otherwise.

## Challenge 85

Write a program that stores employee records in a file. The program should be able to read the records back and display them on the screen.

## Solution

```
// Project: chall85
// Record IO
#include <fstream>
#include <iostream>
using namespace std ;

int main( )
{
    struct employee
    {
        char name[ 20 ] ;
        int age ;
        float basic ;
        float gross ;
    } ;
    employee e ;
```

```
char ch = 'Y' ;

// create file for output
ofstream outfile ;
outfile.open ( "EMPLOYEE.DAT", ios::out | ios::binary ) ;

while ( ch == 'Y' || ch == 'y' )
{
    cout << "Enter a record:" ;
    cin >> e.name >> e.age >> e.basic >> e.gross ;
    outfile.write ( ( char * ) &e, sizeof ( e ) ) ;
    cout << "Add another Y/N? " ;
    cin >> ch ;
}

outfile.close( ) ;

// create file for input
ifstream infile ;
infile.open ( "EMPLOYEE.DAT", ios::in | ios::binary ) ;

while ( infile.read ( ( char * ) &e, sizeof ( e ) ) )
{
    cout << e.name << '\t' << e.age << '\t'
        << e.basic << '\t' << e.gross << endl ;
}
return 0 ;
}
```

## Sample Run

```
Enter a record Saurabh 25 4500 7600
Add another Y/N? Y
Enter a record Santosh 26 6500 9300
Add another Y/N? Y
Enter a record Sameer 30 5400 8250
Add another Y/N? N

Saurabh 25    4500   7600
Santosh 26    6500   9300
Sameer  30    5400   8250
```

## Explanation

On execution the program asks the user to enter employee records. Each record entered is written to disk using the **ofstream::write( )** function. Once all the records are written the file is closed. The same file is then opened for reading in binary mode and it is read record by record. Every record read is displayed on the screen.

We have used two functions here: **write( )**, a member of **ofstream**; and **read( )**, a member of **ifstream**. These functions think about data in terms of bytes. They don't care how the data is formatted, they simply transfer a buffer full of bytes from and to a disk file. Consider the call to **write( )**.

outfile.write ( ( char * ) &e, sizeof ( e ) ) ;

Here we are trying to tell **write( )** to write everything from the address given by **&e** up to the next **sizeof ( e )** bytes. Note that it is necessary to cast the address passed to **write( )** into a **char \***, since **write( )** doesn't know about an **employee \***.

The parameters passed to **read( )** are identical to the ones passed to **write( )**—the address of the data buffer and its length in bytes.

# 15 / Total Challenges: 4

# Template Challenges

**T**emplates is a source code level code reuse mechanism. It lets us write generalized functions and classes. Once written, based on the requirement, the compiler can generate specific functions and classes from them. This is an extremely useful tool that helps write code such that it gets reused rather than reinvented. This chapter tests your understanding of this important tool.

## Challenge 86

Write a program that implements an **Array** class using templates. Use the **Array** class to maintain an array of integers and an array of floats.

### Solution

```
// Project: chall86
// Templated Array c
#include <iostream>
using namespace std ;

// Templated Array class having elements of type T
template <class T>
class Array
{
    private :

        int len ;
        T *ptr ;

    public :

        Array( )
        {
            len = 0 ;
            ptr = 0 ;
        }

        Array ( int l )
        {
            ptr = new T[ l ] ;
            len = l ;
        }

        ~Array( )
        {
            delete[ ] ptr ;
        }
```

```
        void erase( )
        {
            delete [ ] ptr ;
            ptr = 0 ;
            len = 0 ;
        }

        T& operator[ ] ( int index )
        {
            return ptr[ index ] ;
        }

        int getLength( )
        {
            return len ;
        }
} ;

int main( )
{
    Array <int> arr1 ( 10 ) ;
    Array <float> arr2 ( 10 ) ;
    int i ;

    for ( i = 0 ; i < 10 ; i++ )
    {
        arr1[ i ] = i ;
        arr2[ i ] = i + 0.5 ;
    }

    for ( i = 0 ; i < 10 ; i++ )
        cout << arr1[ i ] << "\t" << arr2[ i ] << endl ;

    cout << "Lengths = " << arr1.getLength( ) << "\t"
            << arr2.getLength( ) << endl ;
    arr1.erase( ) ;
    arr2.erase( ) ;
    cout << "Lengths = " << arr1.getLength( ) << "\t"
            << arr2.getLength( ) << endl ;
```

```
        return 0 ;
}
```

```
0    0.5
1    1.5
2    2.5
3    3.5
4    4.5
5    5.5
6    6.5
7    7.5
8    8.5
9    9.5
Lengths = 10    10
Lengths = 0     0
```

## Explanation

The template **Array** class works on a generic type **T**. During compilation from the generic **Array** class, two specific classes would be created—one that works on an integer array and another that works on a float array. How does the compiler decide that these two versions should be created? Well, from the definitions of **arr1** and **arr2** in **main( )**.

Once we have created the two arrays, we have populated them with some values. To do this we have overloaded the **[ ]** operator that helps us access individual element of an array.

The **erase( )** function vacates the array, whereas, **getLength( )** reports the current length of the array.

## Challenge   87

Write a template function **myswap( )** that interchanges contents of two variables. Use it to swap integers, floats, long integers and strings.

Can this function be given a name **swap( )** instead of **myswap( )**?

## Solution

```
// Project: chall87
// Templated myswap( ) function
# include <iostream>
using namespace std ;

template <class T>
void myswap ( T& a, T& b )
{
    T c ;

    c = a ;
    a = b ;
    b = c ;
}

int main( )
{
    int  x = 10, y = 20 ;
    float  i = 1.5, j = 2.5 ;
    double  u = 10.23, v = 20.45 ;
    string str1 = "Mumbai", str2 = "Nagpur" ;

    cout << "Before swapping:" << endl ;
    cout << "x = " << x << "\t" << "y = " << y << endl ;
    cout << "i = " << i << "\t" << "j = " << j << endl ;
    cout << "u = " << u << "\t" << "v = " << v << endl ;
    cout << "str1 = " << str1 << "\t" << "str2 = " << str2 << endl ;

    myswap ( x, y ) ;
    myswap ( i, j ) ;
    myswap ( u, v ) ;
    myswap ( str1, str2 ) ;

    cout << "After swapping:" << endl ;
    cout << "x = " << x << "\t" << "y = " << y << endl ;
    cout << "i = " << i << "\t" << "j = " << j << endl ;
    cout << "u = " << u << "\t" << "v = " << v << endl ;
```

```
        cout << "str1 = " << str1 << "\t" << "str2 = " << str2 << endl ;
}
```

## Sample Run

Before swapping:
x = 10  y = 20
i = 1.5 j = 2.5
u = 10.23      v = 20.45
str1 = Mumbai   str2 = Nagpur
After swapping:
x = 20  y = 10
i = 2.5 j = 1.5
u = 20.45      v = 10.23
str1 = Nagpur   str2 = Mumbai

## Explanation

Four versions of **myswap( )** function are created by the compiler based on our generic version of **myswap( )**. There is nothing specific about **T**, we can use any other name in its place.

We cannot use the name **swap( )** instead of **myswap( )** because Standard Template Library already has a function by that name and may create conflict.

## Challenge 88

Write a program that has a templated **Queue** class, which implements the Queue data structure. Additions to the queue should happen at the rear end, whereas, deletions should happen from the front end. Make provision to check whether queue is full before adding a new element and whether queue is empty before removing an existing element from it.

## Solution

```
// Project: chall88
// Templated Queue implementation
#include <iostream>
using namespace std ;

const int MAX = 3 ;

template <class T>
class Queue
{
    private :

        int front, rear ;
        T a[ MAX ] ;

    public :

        Queue( )
        {
            front = rear = -1 ;
        }

        bool isEmpty( )
        {
            if ( rear == -1 )
                return true ;
            else
                return false ;
        }

        bool isFull( )
        {
            if ( rear == MAX - 1 )
                return true ;
            else
                return false ;
        }
```

```cpp
        void add ( int n )
        {
            rear++ ;
            a[ rear ] = n ;

            if ( front == -1 )
                front = 0 ;
        }

        int del( )
        {
            int n ;

            n = a[ front ] ;
            if ( front == rear )
                front = rear = -1 ;
            else
                front++ ;

            return n ;
        }
} ;

int main( )
{
    Queue <int > intq ;
    int n ;

    if ( !intq.isFull( ) )
    {
        intq.add ( 10 ) ;
        cout << "Element 10 added to queue" << endl ;
    }
    else
        cout << "Queue is full" << endl ;

    if ( !intq.isFull( ) )
    {
        intq.add ( 20 ) ;
        cout << "Element 20 added to queue" << endl ;
    }
```

```
else
    cout << "Queue is full" << endl ;

if ( !intq.isFull( ) )
{
    intq.add ( 30 ) ;
    cout << "Element 30 added to queue" << endl ;
}
else
    cout << "Queue is full" << endl ;

if ( !intq.isFull( ) )
{
    intq.add ( 40 ) ;
    cout << "Element 40 added to queue" << endl ;
}
else
    cout << "Queue is full" << endl ;

if ( !intq.isEmpty( ) )
{
    n = intq.del( ) ;
    cout << "Element deleted from queue = " << n << endl ;
}
else
    cout << "Queue is empty" << endl ;

if ( !intq.isEmpty( ) )
{
    n = intq.del( ) ;
    cout << "Element deleted from queue = " << n << endl ;
}
else
    cout << "Queue is empty" << endl ;

if ( !intq.isEmpty( ) )
{
    n = intq.del( ) ;
    cout << "Element deleted from queue = " << n << endl ;
}
else
```

```
        cout << "Queue is empty" << endl ;

    if ( !intq.isEmpty( ) )
    {
        n = intq.del( ) ;
        cout << "Element deleted from queue = " << n << endl ;
    }
    else
        cout << "Queue is empty" << endl ;
}
```

## Sample Run

```
Element 10 added to queue
Element 20 added to queue
Element 30 added to queue
Queue is full
Element deleted from queue = 10
Element deleted from queue = 20
Element deleted from queue = 30
Queue is empty
```

## Explanation

Queue is a FIFO list—the first element that joins the queue is the first one that gets removed from it. The template class ensures that we can easily use the same class to maintain a queue of floats / doubles / strings, etc.

If the queue is empty both **front** and **rear** have a value -1. The function **isEmpty( )** checks whether the queue is empty. If it is, then we cannot remove an element from it. Likewise, the **isFull( )** function checks whether the queue is full. If it is, we cannot add a new element to it.

## Challenge 89

Write a program that has a templated **Stack** class, which implements the Stack data structure. Both additions and deletions to the stack should happen at the same end called **top**. Make provision to check whether stack is full before adding a new element and whether stack is empty before removing an existing element from it.

## Solution

```
// Project: chall89
// Templated Stack implementation
#include <iostream>
using namespace std ;

const int MAX = 3 ;

template <class T>
class Stack
{
    private :

        int top ;
        T a[ MAX ] ;

    public :

        Stack( )
        {
            top = -1 ;
        }

        void push ( int x )
        {
            top++ ;
            a[ top ] = x ;
        }

        int pop( )
        {
            int n ;

            n = a[ top ] ;
            top-- ;
```

```
            return n ;
        }

        bool isEmpty( )
        {
            if ( top == -1 )
                return true ;
            else
                return false ;
        }

        bool isFull( )
        {
            if ( top == MAX - 1 )
                return true ;
            else
                return false ;
        }
} ;

int main( )
{
    Stack <int> s ;
    int n ;

    if ( !s.isFull( ) )
    {
        s.push ( 10 ) ;
        cout << "Element 10 added to stack" << endl ;
    }
    else
        cout << "Stack is full" << endl ;

    if ( !s.isFull( ) )
    {
        s.push ( 20 ) ;
        cout << "Element 20 added to stack" << endl ;
    }
    else
        cout << "Stack is full" << endl ;
```

```
if ( !s.isFull( ) )
{
    s.push ( 30 ) ;
    cout << "Element 30 added to stack" << endl ;
}
else
    cout << "Stack is full" << endl ;

if ( !s.isFull( ) )
{
    s.push ( 40 ) ;
    cout << "Element 40 added to stack" << endl ;
}
else
    cout << "Stack is full" << endl ;

if ( !s.isEmpty( ) )
{
    n = s.pop( ) ;
    cout << "Element popped from stack = " << n << endl ;
}
else
    cout << "Stack is empty" << endl ;

if ( !s.isEmpty( ) )
{
    n = s.pop( ) ;
    cout << "Element popped from stack = " << n << endl ;
}
else
    cout << "Stack is empty" << endl ;

if ( !s.isEmpty( ) )
{
    n = s.pop( ) ;
    cout << "Element popped from stack = " << n << endl ;
}
else
    cout << "Stack is empty" << endl ;

if ( !s.isEmpty( ) )
```

```
{
    n = s.pop( ) ;
    cout << "Element popped from stack = " << n << endl ;
}
else
    cout << "Stack is empty" << endl ;
}
```

## Sample Run

Element 10 added to stack
Element 20 added to stack
Element 30 added to stack
Stack is full
Element popped from stack = 30
Element popped from stack = 20
Element popped from stack = 10
Stack is empty

## Explanation

Stack is a LIFO list—the last element that is pushed (added) to the stack is the first one that gets popped (removed) from it. The template class ensures that we can easily use the same class to maintain a stack of floats / doubles / strings, etc.

If the stack is empty **top** has a value -1. The function **isEmpty( )** checks whether the stack is empty. If it is, then we cannot pop an element from it. Likewise the **isFull( )** function checks whether the stack is full. If it is, we cannot push a new element to it.

# 16 / Total Challenges: 4

# Exception Handling Challenges

Exceptions are errors that occur at run time. There are numerous reasons why exceptions occur, like falling short of memory, inability to open a file, exceeding the bounds of an array, attempting to initialize an object to an impossible value, etc. This chapter tests whether you are able to handle such exceptional situations in the C++ way.

YASHAVANT & ADITYA KANETKAR'S

101 **Challenges** In C++ Programming

Solve 101 Challenges to hone C++ Programming skills
Practise them to be a mature C++ programmer

## Challenge 90

Write a program that creates a **vector** of 10 elements, and sets up a value in it at a position **index**, received from keyboard. Also, resize the **vector** to a new bigger size. Create a **bitset** of 5 bits and set it up with a binary string received from keyboard. Create another **bitset**, set it up with 0s and 1s and convert this string into an **unsigned long int**. While carrying out all these operations take care of exceptional conditions that may occur during execution.

## Solution

```
// Project: chall90
// Standard exceptions demo
#include <iostream>
#include <bitset>
#include <string>
#include <vector>
using namespace std ;

int main( )
{
    vector < int > arr ( 10 ) ;
    int index ;

    cout << "Enter vector index: " << endl ;
    cin >> index ;

    try
    {
        arr.at ( index ) = 100 ;
        arr.resize ( arr.max_size( ) + 1 ) ;
    }
    catch ( const out_of_range& oor )
    {
        cout << "Out of Range error: " << oor.what( ) << endl ;
    }
    catch ( const length_error& le )
    {
```

```
        cout << "Length error: " << le.what() << endl ;
    }

    string str ;
    cout << "Enter a string containing 0s and 1s: " << endl ;
    cin >> str ;

    try
    {
        bitset < 5 > bs1 ( str ) ;
        bitset < 33 > bs2 ;
        bs2[ 32 ] = 1 ;
        bs2[ 0 ] = 1 ;
        unsigned long x = bs2.to_ulong( ) ;
    }
    catch ( const invalid_argument& ia )
    {
        cout << "Invalid argument: " << ia.what( ) << endl ;
    }
    catch ( exception &e )
    {
        cout << "Unknown exception" << e.what( ) << endl ;
    }

    return 0 ;
}
```

## Sample Runs

```
Enter vector index:
4
Length error: vector::_M_default_append
Enter a string containing 0s and 1s:
0101
Unknown exception_Base_bitset::_M_do_to_ulong

Enter vector index:
20
Out of Range error: vector::_M_range_check: __n (which is 20) >= this-
>size() (which is 10)
Enter a string containing 0s and 1s:
```

1102
Invalid argument: bitset::_M_copy_from_ptr

## Explanation

With regards to **vector**, we have caught two standard exceptions—one that occurs when we try to access a **vector** element beyond its range, and another that occurs while resizing the **vector**. These exceptions are called out of range exception and length error exception, respectively.

With regards to **bitset** we have caught two exceptions—one that occurs when we provide an invalid string to convert into a **bitset**, and another that occurs while converting a **bitset** into an **unsigned long int**.

When we do not know which exception is likely to occur, we can write a catch all block using the base class of all standard exceptions, namely **exception** class.

## Challenge 91

Write a program that implements a Queue class, which throws an exception if we attempt to add a new element to a queue that is already full, or we try to delete an element from a queue that is already empty. Tackle these exceptions in **main( )**.

## Solution

```
// Project: chall91
// User-defined exception class
#include <iostream>
#include <string>
using namespace std ;

class fullorempty
{
    public :

        string str ;
```

```
        fullorempty ( string s )
        {
            str = s ;
        }
} ;

class queue
{
    private :

        static const int MAX = 4 ;
        int arr[ MAX ] ;
        int front, rear ;

    public :

        queue( )
        {
            front = -1 ;
            rear = -1 ;
        }

        void addq ( int item )
        {
            if ( rear == MAX - 1 )
                throw fullorempty ( "Queue is full" ) ;

            rear++ ;
            arr[ rear ] = item ;

            if ( front == -1 )
                front = 0 ;
        }

        int delq( )
        {
            int data ;

            if ( front == -1 )
                throw fullorempty ( "Queue is empty" ) ;
```

```
            data = arr[ front ] ;
            if ( front == rear )
                front = rear = -1 ;
            else
                front++ ;

            return data ;
        }
} ;

int main( )
{
    queue a ;

    try
    {
        a.addq ( 11 ) ;
        cout << "Added 11" << endl ;
        a.addq ( 12 ) ;
        cout << "Added 12" << endl ;
        a.addq ( 13 ) ;
        cout << "Added 13" << endl ;
        a.addq ( 14 ) ;
        cout << "Added 15" << endl ;
        a.addq ( 15 ) ; // oops, queue is full
    }
    catch ( fullorempty fe )
    {
        cout << endl << fe.str << endl ;
    }

    int i ;
    try
    {
        i = a.delq( ) ;
        cout << endl << "Item deleted = " << i ;
        i = a.delq( ) ;
        cout << endl << "Item deleted = " << i ;
        i = a.delq( ) ;
        cout << endl << "Item deleted = " << i ;
        i = a.delq( ) ;
```

```
            cout << endl << "Item deleted = " << i ;
            i = a.delq( ) ; // oops, queue is empty
            cout << endl << "Item deleted = " << i ;
        }
    catch ( fullorempty fe )
    {
            cout << endl << fe.str << endl ;
    }

    return 0 ;
}
```

## Sample Run

```
Added 11
Added 12
Added 13
Added 15

Queue is full

Item deleted = 11
Item deleted = 12
Item deleted = 13
Item deleted = 14
Queue is empty
```

## Explanation

In our program we have purposefully created two statements that cause exceptions. The first,

a.addq ( 15 ) ; // oops, queue is full

causes the **fullorempty** exception to be thrown resulting in the message 'Queue is full' being displayed.

Similarly the statement,

i = a.delq( ) ; // oops, queue is empty right now

causes the exception **fullorempty** to be thrown, resulting in the message 'Queue is empty' being displayed.

When the exceptions are thrown an exception class object gets created through the constructor of the exception class (in this case the **fullorempty** class). When the constructor is called we pass it a message. It copies this message into a **public** member (**str**) of the exception class. The **catch** blocks access this **public** member and prints the relevant message.

## Challenge 92

Write a program sets up a termination handler. The handler should get called when an unknown exception occurs. The handler should terminate program execution.

## Solution

```
// Project: chall92
// Termination handler
#include <iostream>
#include <exception>
#include <cstdlib>
#include <vector>

using namespace std ;

void myfun( )
{
    cout << "Terminate handler called" << endl ;
    abort( ) ;
}

int main( )
{
    set_terminate ( myfun ) ;

    vector < int > arr ( 10 ) ;
    int index ;
```

```
        cout << "Enter vector index: " << endl ;
        cin >> index ;

        try
        {
            arr.at ( index ) = 100 ;
        }
        catch ( exception e )
        {
            cout << "Unknown exception... terminating" << endl ;
            throw "Unknown exception" ;
        }

        cout << "Control reached here" << endl ;

        return 0 ;
}
```

## Sample Runs

Enter vector index:
5
Control reached here


Enter vector index:
15
Unknown exception... terminating
Terminate handler called

## Explanation

During the first run since the index 5 is well within the range of the vector **arr** there is no exception. In such a case control reaches beyond the **catch** block and displays the message 'Control reached here'.

During the second run since the **index** 15 exceeds the bounds of the Vector **arr** whose size has been set to 10, an exception occurs. Since we have set up the terminate handler, when we throw "Unknown exception" the terminate handler **myfunc( )** gets called. This handler aborts the execution by calling the C library function **abort( )**. For this function to work we have included the file 'cstdlib'.

## Challenge  93

What happens to the objects created in try block when an exception occurs and control is transferred to the catch block? Can we write a catchall like catch block that will catch any exception that we haven't caught specifically?

## Solution

```cpp
// Project: chall93
// Catchall block
#include <iostream>
#include <fstream>
#include <vector>
using namespace std ;

class Sample
{
    public :

        Sample( )
        {
            cout << "Constructor of Sample " << endl ;
        }

        ~Sample( )
        {
            cout << "Destructor of Sample "  << endl ;
        }
} ;

int main( )
{
    try
    {
```

```
        Sample s1, s2 ;
        vector < int > arr ( 10 ) ;

        arr.at ( 5 ) = 100 ;

        ifstream infile ( "ABC.XYZ" ) ;
        if ( infile.fail( ) )
            throw "Error in opening file" ;
    }
    catch ( const out_of_range& oor )
    {
        cout << "Out of Range error: " << oor.what( ) << endl ;
    }
    catch ( ... )
    {
        cout << "Default Exception\n";
    }

  return 0 ;
}
```

## Sample Run

```
Constructor of Sample
Constructor of Sample
Destructor of Sample
Destructor of Sample
Default Exception
```

## Explanation

When an exception occurs and control is transferred to the catch block, the objects created in the try block are destroyed. That is why for **s1** and **s2** the destructor got called when we threw an exception when we could not open the file "ABC.XYZ" for reading.

Since we have no catch block that can receive a string being thrown the control is transferred to the catchall block **catch ( ... )**.

# 17/ Total Challenges: 4

# STL Challenges

**W**hile programming we often create a collection of either standard data types or user-defined data types. The typical operations that we carry out on this collection are addition, deletion, walking through the collection, searching, sorting etc. STL allows us to create the collection in a generic manner and then perform the operations on it also in a generic manner. This avoids lot of repetition of code. This chapter presents challenges related to the STL theme.

## Challenge 94

Write a program to maintain a collection of objects of user-defined class **Point**.

## Solution

```
// Project: chall94
// Vector based collection
#include <vector>
#include <iostream>
using namespace std ;

class Point
{
    public :

        int x, y ;

        Point ( int xx = 0 , int yy = 0 )
        {
            x = xx ;
            y = yy ;
        }

        Point ( const Point& pt )
        {
            x = pt.x ;
            y = pt.y ;
        }

        virtual ~Point( )
        {
        }

        Point& operator = ( const Point& pt )
        {
            x = pt.x ;
            y = pt.y ;
```

```
                return *this ;
        }

} ;

int main( )
{
    vector <Point> vp1 ;
    vector <Point>::iterator itr ;
    Point *p ;

    for ( int i = 0 ; i < 5 ; i ++ )
    {
        p = new Point ( i + 1, i + 1 ) ;
        vp1.insert ( vp1.end( ), *p ) ;
        delete p ;
    }

    cout << "Vector vp1:" << endl ;
    for ( itr = vp1.begin( ) ; itr != vp1.end( ) ; itr++ )
        cout << "x, y = " << itr->x << ", " << itr->y << endl ;


    cout << "Front: x, y = " ;
    cout << vp1.front( ).x << ", " << vp1.front( ).y << endl ;
    cout << "Back : x, y = " ;
    cout << vp1.back( ).x << ", " << vp1.back( ).y << endl ;

    vector <Point>::reverse_iterator ritr ;
    cout << "Reverse Vector vp1:" << endl ;
    for ( ritr = vp1.rbegin( ) ; ritr != vp1.rend( ) ; ritr++ )
        cout << "x, y = " << ritr->x << ", " << ritr->y << endl ;


    cout << "Sizeof vp1 : " << vp1.size( ) << endl ;

    vector <Point> vp2 ;

    vp2.assign ( vp1.begin( ), vp1.begin( ) + 3 ) ;

    cout << "Vector vp2:" << endl ;
```

```
    for ( itr = vp2.begin( ) ; itr != vp2.end( ) ; itr++ )
        cout << "x, y = " << itr->x << ", " << itr->y << endl ;
    return 0 ;
}
```

## Sample Run

```
Vector vp1:
x, y = 1, 1
x, y = 2, 2
x, y = 3, 3
x, y = 4, 4
x, y = 5, 5
Front: x, y = 1, 1
Back : x, y = 5, 5
Reverse Vector vp1:
x, y = 5, 5
x, y = 4, 4
x, y = 3, 3
x, y = 2, 2
x, y = 1, 1
Sizeof vp1 : 5
Vector vp2:
x, y = 1, 1
x, y = 2, 2
x, y = 3, 3
```

## Explanation

In this program we have first declared a **Point** class containing a constructor, destructor, copy constructor and overloaded assignment operator. Then, in **main( )**, in a **for** loop we have created 5 **Point** objects and added them to the vector **vp**. The addition is done by calling the **insert( )** function of the vector class.

Next, we have iterated through the vector, using the iterator, printing values of all **Point** objects present in the vector. We have also accessed the elements at the beginning and at the end of the vector using the methods **front( )** and **back( )**.

The container can also be walked in the reverse direction using the **reverse_iterator**. Size of the container can be obtained using the **size( )** method. In the end, we have created another vector **vp2** and copied first 3 elements of **vp1** into it and then iterated through **vp2** from beginning to end.

## Challenge  95

Write a program using STL to maintain a Linked List of **Point** objects.

## Solution

```
// Project: chall95
// STL based linked list
#include <stdio.h>
#include <list>
#include <iostream>

using namespace std ;

class Point
{
    public :

        int x, y ;

        Point ( int xx = 0 , int yy = 0 )
        {
            x = xx ;
            y = yy ;
        }

        Point ( const Point& pt )
        {
            x = pt.x ;
            y = pt.y ;
        }
```

```
            virtual ~Point( )
            {
            }

            Point& operator = ( const Point& pt )
            {
                x = pt.x ;
                y = pt.y ;
                return *this ;
            }
} ;

int main( )
{
    list <Point> li ;
    list <Point>::iterator itr ;
    Point *p ;
    int i ;

    for ( i = 0 ; i < 5 ; i ++ )
    {
        p = new Point( i + 1, i + 1 ) ;
        li.insert ( li.end( ), *p ) ;
        delete p ;
    }

    cout << "List li: " << endl ;
    for ( itr = li.begin( ) ; itr != li.end( ) ; itr++ )
        cout << "x, y = " << itr->x << ", " << itr->y << endl ;

    return 0 ;
}
```

## Sample Run

List li:
x, y = 1, 1
x, y = 2, 2
x, y = 3, 3
x, y = 4, 4
x, y = 5, 5

## Explanation

Here we have created 5 **Point** objects and inserted them at the end of a linked list using the **insert( )** function of the templated **list** class of STL.

Then using the iterator we have walked through the linked list, printing values of each **Point** object in turn.

## Challenge  96

Write a program using STL to maintain a telephone book containing names and telephone numbers. It should be possible to search the telephone book either using a name or using a telephone number.

## Solution

```
// Project: chall96
// Telephone book using STL
#include <iostream>
#include <vector>
#include <string>
#include <cstdlib>
using namespace std ;

struct Person
{
    string name ;
    int phoneNum ;

    Person ( string s = "", int num = 0 )
    {
        name = s ;
        phoneNum = num ;
    }
} ;

void displayData ( vector <Person>& ) ;
void search ( vector <Person>&, string ) ;
```

```
void search ( vector <Person>&, int ) ;

int main( )
{
    vector <Person> p ;
    int ch ;
    string str ;
    int num ;

    p.push_back ( Person ( "Nimish", 2534123 ) ) ;
    p.push_back ( Person ( "Anmol", 982301 ) ) ;
    p.push_back ( Person ( "Shubham", 789635 ) ) ;

    while ( 1 )
    {
        cout << "1. View Phone Book" << endl ;
        cout << "2. Search by name" << endl ;
        cout << "3. Search by number" << endl ;
        cout << "0. Exit" << endl ;
        cout << "Enter your choice" << endl ;

        cin >> ch ;

        switch ( ch )
        {
            case 1 :
                displayData ( p ) ;
                break ;

            case 2 :
                cout << "Enter name: " << endl ;
                cin >> str ;
                search ( p, str ) ;
                break ;

            case 3 :
                cout << "Enter phone number: " << endl ;
                cin >> num ;
                search ( p, num ) ;
                break ;
```

```
                case 0 :
                    exit ( 1 ) ;

                default:
                    cout << "Invalid choice" << endl ;
            }
        }
        return 0 ;
    }

void displayData ( vector< Person >& p )
{
    if ( p.size( ) == 0 )
    {
        cout << "No data in the phone book" << endl ;
        return ;
    }

    for ( int i = 0 ; i < p.size( ) ; i++ )
        cout << p[ i ].name << " " << p[ i ].phoneNum << endl ;

    cout << endl ;
}

void search ( vector< Person >& p, string str )
{
    bool found = false ;
    cout << "Search Results: " << endl ;

    for ( int i = 0 ; i < p.size( ) ; i++ )
    {
        if ( str == p[ i ].name )
        {
            found = true ;
            cout << p[ i ].name << " " << p[ i ].phoneNum ;
            cout << endl << endl ;
        }
    }

    if ( found == false )
        cout << "No matching entry" << endl << endl ;
```

```
}
void search ( vector <Person>& p, int num )
{
    bool found = false ;
    cout << "Search Results: " << endl ;

    for ( int i = 0 ; i < p.size( ) ; i++ )
    {
        if ( num == p[ i ].phoneNum )
        {
            found = true ;
            cout << p[ i ].name << " " << p[ i ].phoneNum ;
            cout << endl << endl ;
        }
    }

    if ( found == false )
        cout << "No matching entry" << endl << endl ;
}
```

## Sample Run

```
1. View Phone Book
2. Search by name
3. Search by number
0. Exit
Enter your choice
1
Nimish 2534123
Anmol 982301
Shubham 789635

1. View Phone Book
2. Search by name
3. Search by number
0. Exit
Enter your choice
2
Enter name:
Dinesh
```

Search Results:
No matching entry

1. View Phone Book
2. Search by name
3. Search by number
0. Exit
Enter your choice
2
Enter name:
Anmol
Search Results:
Anmol 982301

1. View Phone Book
2. Search by name
3. Search by number
0. Exit
Enter your choice
3
Enter phone number:
123456
Search Results:
No matching entry

1. View Phone Book
2. Search by name
3. Search by number
0. Exit
Enter your choice
3
Enter phone number:
789635
Search Results:
Shubham 789635

1. View Phone Book
2. Search by name
3. Search by number
0. Exit
Enter your choice

0

## Explanation

Here we have created 3 **Person** objects and inserted them in a vector using the **push_back( )** function of the templated **vector** class of STL.

Then, through a menu we have listed all existing contacts in the telephone book and searched the telephone book by name or by telephone number.

## Challenge   97

Write a program that uses bitset STL container to carry out following operations:

Set up a bit-pattern of desired size and value

Count number of 0s and 1s in a bit pattern

Check whether any bit in a bit-pattern is set or not

Set a specific value at a desired position in a bit-pattern

Flip individual or all the bits in a bit-pattern

Reset individual or all the bits in a bit-pattern

Obtain binary equivalent of a decimal number

## Solution

```
// Project: chall97
// Demonstrates usage of bitset
#include <bits/stdc++.h>
using namespace std ;

const int M = 8 ;

int main( )
{
```

```
// 3 ways to set a bit pattern in a bitset
bitset<M> bs1 ;  // sets all 0s
bitset<M> bs2 ( 45 ) ; // sets binary equivalent of 45
bitset<M> bs3 ( "00101100" ) ;  // sets the given binary pattern
bitset<M> bs4 ( "00000000" ) ;  // sets the given binary pattern
bitset<M> bs5 ( "11111111" ) ;  // sets the given binary pattern

cout << "bs1 = " << bs1 << endl ;
cout << "bs2 = " << bs2 << endl ;
cout << "bs3 = " << bs3 << endl ;
cout << "bs4 = " << bs4 << endl ;
cout << "bs5 = " << bs5 << endl ;

int numof1s, numof0s ;

numof1s = bs3.count( ) ;
numof0s = bs3.size( ) - numof1s ;

cout << "Number of 1s in bs3 = " << numof1s << endl ;
cout << "Number of 0s in bs3 = " << numof0s << endl ;

if ( !bs1.any( ) )
    cout << "bs1 has no bit set" << endl ;

if ( !bs5.none( ) )
    cout << "bs5 has all bit set" << endl ;

bs1.set( ) ; // sets all bits
cout << "bs1 after setting all bits = " << bs1 << endl ;

// set pattern 00001111
bs4.set ( 0 ) ; // or bs4[ 0 ] = 1
bs4.set ( 1 ) ; // or bs4[ 1 ] = 1
bs4.set ( 2 ) ; // or bs4[ 2 ] = 1
bs4.set ( 3 ) ; // or bs4[ 3 ] = 1

bs4.set ( 4, 0 ) ; // or bs4[ 4 ] = 0
bs4.set ( 5, 0 ) ; // or bs4[ 5 ] = 0
bs4.set ( 6, 0 ) ; // or bs4[ 6 ] = 0
bs4.set ( 7, 0 ) ; // or bs4[ 6 ] = 0
```

```
    cout << "bs4 after setting 00001111 = " << bs4 << endl ;

    bs4.reset ( 1 ) ; // sets bit 1 to 0
    cout << "bs4 after resetting bit 1 = " << bs4 << endl ;

    bs4.reset( ) ; // sets all bits to 0
    cout << "bs4 after resetting all bits = " << bs4 << endl ;

    int val ;
    val = bs4.test ( 2 ) ;
    if ( val )
        cout << "2nd bit is bs4 is on" << endl ;
    else
        cout << "2nd bit is bs4 is off" << endl ;

    cout << "Current bs4 value = " << bs4 << endl ;
    bs4.flip ( 3 ) ;
    cout << "bs4 after flipping bit 3 = " << bs4 << endl ;

    bs4.flip( ) ;
    cout << "bs4 after flipping all bits = " << bs4 << endl ;

    // Converting decimal number to binary by using bitset
    int num = 65 ;
    cout << "Decimal number = " << num << endl ;
    cout << "Binary equivalent = " << bitset<8> ( num ) ;

    return 0 ;
}
```

## Sample Run

```
bs1 = 00000000
bs2 = 00101101
bs3 = 00101100
bs4 = 00000000
bs5 = 11111111
Number of 1s in bs3 = 3
Number of 0s in bs3 = 5
bs1 has no bit set
bs5 has all bit set
```

bs1 after setting all bits = 11111111
bs4 after setting 00001111 = 00001111
bs4 after resetting bit 1 = 00001101
bs4 after resetting all bits = 00000000
2nd bit is bs4 is off
Current bs4 value = 00000000
bs4 after flipping bit 3 = 00001000
bs4 after flipping all bits = 11110111
Decimal number = 65
Binary equivalent = 01000001

## Explanation

The program is self-explanatory. Do take a look at the comments and corroborate it with the output shown in the Sample Run of the program.

# 18 / Total Challenges: 4

# Miscellaneous Challenges

There are certain features in C++ that you would need less frequently. These include smart pointers, pointers to members and typecasting. This chapter poses challenges in these features of C++ programming

YASHAVANT & ADITYA KANETKAR'S

# 101 Challenges

## In C++ Programming

Solve 101 Challenges to hone C++ Programming skills
Practise them to be a mature C++ programmer

## Challenge  98

Write a program that maintains a linked list using a **Container** class. Also implement a **SmartPointer** class that lets you access **Container** elements using the * operator and lets you iterate through the **Container** using the ++ operator.

### Solution

```
// Project: chall98
// Smart pointer to iterate through a container
#include <iostream>
using namespace std ;

class Container
{
    private :

        struct node
        {
            int data ;
            node *link ;
        } *head, *current ;

        int count ;

    public :

        Container( )
        {
            head = current = NULL ;
            count = 0 ;
        }

        void add ( int n )
        {
            node *temp = new node ;
            temp -> data = n ;
            temp -> link = NULL ;
```

```
                    if ( head == NULL )
                        head = current = temp ;
                    else
                    {
                        node *q ;
                        q = head ;

                        while ( q -> link != NULL )
                            q = q -> link ;

                        q -> link = temp ;
                    }

                    count++ ;
                }

                int getcount( )
                {
                    return count ;
                }

                friend class SmartPointer ;
} ;

class SmartPointer
{
    private :

        Container *cptr ;

    public :

        SmartPointer ( Container *t )
        {
            cptr = t ;
        }

        int operator *( )
        {
            if ( cptr->current == NULL )
```

```
                        return NULL ;
                else
                {
                        int i = cptr->current->data ;
                        return i ;
                }
        }

        void operator ++ ( int n )
        {
                if ( cptr->current != NULL )
                        cptr->current = cptr->current->link ;
        }

} ;

int main( )
{
        Container c ;

        c.add ( 10 ) ;
        c.add ( 20 ) ;
        c.add ( 0 ) ;
        c.add ( -40 ) ;
        c.add ( 50 ) ;

        SmartPointer sptr ( &c ) ;

        for ( int i = 0 ; i < c.getcount( ) ; i++ )
        {
                cout << *sptr << endl ;
                sptr++ ;
        }
        return 0 ;
}
```

## Sample Run

```
10
20
0
```

-40
50

## Explanation

A container is a way to organize data in memory. Hence stacks, linked lists, arrays are all containers. An iterator is an object that moves through a container accessing various elements of the container.

We can iterate through an ordinary C++ array by using a pointer. However, with more sophisticated containers plain C++ pointers won't work. If the items stored in a container are not placed in adjacent memory locations, incrementing the pointer becomes complicated. For example, moving to the next node in the linked list doesn't merely involve incrementing a pointer. We have to follow the link to the next node. The solution to this is to create a class of smart pointers.

An object of a smart pointer class wraps its member functions around an ordinary pointer. The + and the * operator are overloaded in this class. So it knows how to tackle situations when the container elements are not in adjacent memory locations. Iterators are thus nothing but objects of the smart pointer class.

In the program the **Container** class implements the linked list. It has three data members: **head, current** and **count**. Of these, **head** and **current** are pointers to nodes, whereas **count** is an integer. The **head** pointer always points to the first node in the linked list. If the linked list is empty **head** contains NULL. As the name suggests **current** always points to the current node in the list. The 'current node' means the one which would be returned if we say **\*current**. **count** keeps track of the number of nodes in the linked list. Every time a new node is added, the value of **count** is incremented by *1*.

The **Smartpointer** class has been declared as a **friend** of the **Container** class. This in effect means that all the member functions of the **Smartpointer** class would have an access to the **private** data members of the **Container** class.

In the **Smartpointer** class we have two overloaded operator functions. The **operator \* ( )** function returns the integer in the current node. The **operator ++ ( )** function advances the **current** pointer to point to the next node in the linked list.

In **main( )** we have added nodes to the linked list. Then we have built an object of **Smartpointer** class through the statement

smartpointer sptr ( &c ) ;

The constructor sets up the *container c*'s address being passed to it in a **container** pointer. Using this pointer the member functions can access the **private** data members of the **container**.

The crux of the program is the **for** loop.

```
for ( int i = 0 ; i < c.getcount( ) ; i++ )
{
    cout << endl << *sptr ;
    sptr++ ;
}
```

Here **getcount( )** returns the number of nodes currently in the linked list. **cout << *sptr** invokes the overloaded **operator * ( )** function. This returns the integer contained in the node at which *current* is currently pointing. Through **sptr++** the **operator ++ ( )** function gets called. It moves **current** to make it point to the next node in the linked list.

## Challenge 99

Write a program that implements a **Container** class that maintains an array of **Sample** objects. Create a **SmartPointer** class that would act as a friend of the **Container** class. Overload the -> operator in the **SmartPointer** class such that in **main( )** we can use the **SmartPointer** object like a pointer.

## Solution

```
// Project: chall99
// Overloading of -> operator
#include <iostream>
#include <cstring>
using namespace std ;

class Sample
```

```
{
    private :

        int i ;
        float a ;

    public :

        Sample( )
        {
        }

        Sample ( int ii, float aa )
        {
            i = ii ;
            a = aa ;
        }

        void fun1( )
        {
            cout << i << "\t" << a << endl ;
        }

        void fun2( )
        {
            cout << i * a << endl ;
        }
} ;

class Container
{
    private :

        enum { size = 100 } ;
        Sample *arr[ size ] ;
        int index ;

    public :

        Container( )
        {
```

```
                    index = 0 ;
                    memset ( arr, 0, size * sizeof ( Sample * ) ) ;
                }

                void add ( int ii, float aa )
                {
                    if ( index >= size )
                        return ;

                    arr[ index ] = new Sample ( ii, aa ) ;
                    index++ ;
                }

                friend class SmartPointer ;
            } ;

    class SmartPointer
    {
        private :

                Container *c ;
                int index ;

        public :

                SmartPointer ( Container *pctr )
                {
                    c = pctr ;
                    index = 0 ;
                }

                int operator ++ ( int n )
                {
                    if ( index >= c->size )
                        return 0 ;

                    index++ ;
                    if ( c -> arr[ index ] == 0 )
                        return 0 ;

                    return 1 ;
```

```
        }

        Sample * operator -> ( )
        {
            if ( c -> arr[ index ] )
                return c->arr[ index ] ;

            static Sample dummy ;
            return &dummy ;
        }
} ;

int main( )
{
    Container c ;
    c.add ( 10, 3.14f ) ;
    c.add ( 20, 6.28f ) ;
    c.add ( 30, 9.45f ) ;
    c.add ( 40, 8.66f ) ;

    SmartPointer sptr ( &c ) ;

    do
    {
        sptr->fun1( ) ;
        sptr->fun2( ) ;
    } while ( sptr++ ) ;

    return 0 ;
}
```

## Sample Run

```
10      3.14
31.4
20      6.28
125.6
30      9.45
283.5
40      8.66
346.4
```

## Explanation

Though **sp** is an object we can make it work like a pointer. Moreover, even though **fun1( )** and **fun2( )** are not member functions of the **SmartPointer** class we can still call them in a direct way. The smart pointer mechanism calls those functions for **sample \*** that is returned by the **operator -> ( )** function.

The overloaded **operator ->** is often called a smart pointer operator. Note that the overloaded smart pointer operator must be a member function. Also it must return either an object or its address.

Although the underlying working of the smart pointer is complex, it provides a convenient syntax, which perhaps outweighs the complexity.

## Challenge 100

Write a program to access the structure members using the pointer to member operators, .\* and ->\*.

## Solution

```
// Project: chall100
// Pointer to member operators
#include <iostream>
using namespace std ;

struct sample
{
    int a ;
    float b ;
} ;

int main( )
{
    sample so = { 10, 3.14f } ;

    int sample::*p1 = &sample::a ;
```

```
float sample::*p2 = &sample::b ;

cout << so.*p1 << "\t" << so.*p2 << endl ;

sample *sp ;
sp = &so ;
cout << sp->*p1 << "\t" << sp->*p2 << endl ;

// we can even assign new values
so.*p1 = 20 ;
sp->*p2 = 6.28f ;
cout << so.*p1 << "\t" << so.*p2 << endl ;
cout << sp->*p1 << "\t" << sp->*p2 << endl ;

sample soarr[ ] = {
                        { 30, 9.22f },
                        { 40, 7.33f },
                        { 60, 8.88f }
                };

for ( int i =0 ; i <= 2 ; i++ )
    cout << soarr[ i ].*p1 << "\t" << soarr[ i ].*p2 << endl ;

return 0 ;
}
```

## Sample Run

```
10    3.14
10    3.14
20    6.28
20    6.28
30    9.22
40    7.33
60    8.88
```

## Explanation

To carry out the access and the dereferencing simultaneously, C++ provides two operators: '.*' and '->*'. These are known as pointer to member operators.

Note the definition of the pointers **p1** and **p2**:

```
int sample::*p1 = &sample::a ;
float sample::*p2 = &sample::b
```

Consider the part before the assignment operator. The stars indicate that **p1** and **p2** are pointers. **sample::** indicates they are pointers to an **int** and a **float** within **sample**. We have also initialized these pointers while declaring them, with addresses of **a** and **b** respectively.

Really speaking there is no "address of" **sample::** because we are referring to a class and not to an object of that class. **&sample::a** merely produces an offset into the class. The actual address would be produced when we combine that offset with the starting address of a particular object.

Hence **&sample::a** is nothing more than the syntax of pointer to member. If we use **p1** and **p2** with one object we would get one set of values, if we use it with another we would get another set of values. This is what is shown towards the end of the program, where we have built an array of objects and accessed all objects' elements using **p1** and **p2**. Moral is that the pointers to members are not tied with any specific object.

On the left hand side of '.*' there would always be a structure variable (object) or a reference and on the left hand side of '->*' there would always be a pointer to a structure (object).

## Challenge 101

Write a program that carries out the following conversions using a **static_cast** syntax:

(a)  cast-less conversions
(b)  narrowing conversions
(c)  conversions from **void \***

(d)   implicit type conversions

Also illustrate the use of **reinterpret_cast**.

## Solution

```
#include <iostream>
using namespace std ;

class Base
{
} ;

class Derived : public Base
{
    public :
        operator int( )
        {
            return 1 ;
        }
} ;

class Sample
{
} ;

int main()
{
    int i = 10 ;
    long l ;
    float f ;

    // explicit conversion - safe
    l = static_cast <long> ( i ) ;
    f = static_cast <float> ( i ) ;
    cout << l << "\t" << f << endl ;

    // narrowing conversions
    i = static_cast <int> ( l ) ;
    i = static_cast <int> ( f ) ;
```

```
// dangerous conversion through a void pointer
void *vptr ;
float *fptr ;
vptr = &i ;
fptr = static_cast <float *> ( vptr ) ;

Derived d ;
Base *baseptr ;

// upcasting - safe
baseptr = &d ;

// explicit upcasting - safe
baseptr = static_cast <Base *> ( &d ) ;

int x ;

// conversion through a conversion function
x = d ;
// more explicit conversion through a conversion function
x = static_cast <int> ( d ) ;

int a = 65000 ;
int *iptr = reinterpret_cast <int *> ( a ) ;
cout << iptr << endl ;
iptr++ ;  // increases by four
cout << iptr << endl ;

a = reinterpret_cast <int> ( iptr ) ;
cout << a << endl ;

a++ ;  // increases by 1
cout << a << endl ;

return 0 ;
}
```

## Sample Run

```
10      10
0xfde8
```

```
0xfdec
65004
65005
```

## Explanation

Most of the program is self-explanatory. Take a look at the two statements of the program where we try to cast a pointer to **base** into a pointer to **sample** using **static_cast** an error is flashed. This means that **static_cast** won't allow us to cast out of the hierarchy. However, the traditional C style cast would permit this. This means **static_cast** is safer than traditional casting.

The **reinterpret_cast** can be used to convert pointers to integers or vice versa as shown in the program.

Made in the USA
Monee, IL
17 May 2020

31343023R00174